In *Schools of Character,* Brother Michael Fehrenbach tells the story of Catalyst Schools, a pair of charter public schools that are lifting the lives of students in two of Chicago's most challenging neighborhoods. What makes Catalyst Schools so impressive—aside from their excellent academic results—is their commitment to giving character and values a primary place in the education of students. As Brother Michael expertly relates, Catalyst Schools teach students not just how to learn, but how to live. They draw on the best of multiple educational traditions, offering a free, high-quality, public education infused with lessons in values development and character formation inspired by centuries of Lasallian teaching. *Schools of Character* is a compelling read for anyone who wants to understand how charter public schools are uniquely able to help disadvantaged students thrive academically and build a strong personal foundation for lifelong success—and why these schools are so popular with parents.

—*Nina Rees, President and Chief Executive Officer,*
National Alliance for Public Charter Schools

Many school mission statements speak about educating the whole person but too often focus on the intellectual development of students to the neglect of the other dimensions of our humanity. This work, *Schools of Character,* offers a blueprint for the education of the whole person; a blueprint that is rooted in more than three centuries of practical experience that crosses cultures, ethnicities, and religious traditions. Among other things, it highlights that the education of the young is best accomplished by a community of educators in dialogue with one another; that this community is in relationship with one another and with the students as individuals; and that a student's education takes place outside the classroom as much as it does inside.

Whether teaching in educational institutions with a specific faith tradition, or private academies or public schools, this book presents an educational vision that inculcates fundamental human values so necessary to care for our common home we call Earth.

—*Brother Robert Schieler, FSC,*
Superior General of the Christian Brothers

Dedication

To the dedicated teachers, staff, and administrators who have embraced the Lasallian tradition and who see their work as a vocational commitment to advance the salvation of the young, especially the poor.

Author Acknowledgments

It is important to acknowledge two people in particular, without whom this reflection would not have happened. First of all, Gary Wood asked me to consider writing this book. In spite of my reluctance, he pushed me and encouraged me to put on paper the things that had been in my heart and mind for quite some time. As the book began to take shape, he never stopped being a significant source of encouragement and support. Gary has a deep understanding of the core values explored in the pages of this book. In addition to Gary Wood, Ed Siderewicz has been a source of inspiration for forty years. He has been a companion on the journey into the sacred mystery we call education. His understanding of service with the poor, the value of education as a way beyond economic poverty, and his commitment to the Lasallian tradition have made him a significant friend not only in the process of writing this book but in introducing others to the rich tradition that has inspired schools in eighty countries around the globe. These two men really deserve credit for what follows.

In addition, there are many others who read an initial draft of this work but one stands out as especially important. Brother Miguel Campos has studied the works of Saint John Baptist de La Salle for many years. Miguel's own writings have always been a source of reflection and inspiration. His feedback and encouragement gave me courage to see this project to completion.

My gratitude to these three men and many others is genuine and from the heart. I hope this book offers a little insight into how the charism of Saint John Baptist de La Salle might not just inform our Catholic schools but all educational enterprises, be they religious or state-sponsored.

Finally I would like to thank Saint Mary's Press and Jerry Ruff, my editor, who really made this a book through his expert advice, gift of time, and patience with an inexperienced author.

Schools of Character

Faith-Inspired Public Schools
in the Catholic Lasallian Tradition

Michael Fehrenbach, FSC

saint mary's press

Created by the publishing team of Saint Mary's Press.

Front Cover Image: A Catalyst Schools student concentrates on his studies. (© John Lee, John Lee Pictures ht.)

Back Cover Image: Former Catalyst assistant principal Moses Tighil gathers students for a group photograph in the reading and reflection garden during ceremonies for a memorial brick dedication at Catalyst Howland Charter School. (© Catalyst contributed photo)

Printed in the United States of America

5511

ISBN 978-1-59982-844-2

Contents

Foreword

Imran Shamim
Assistant Director of Information Technology
The Catalyst Schools

In our world where church and state are separate, a religiously affiliated public school is unlawful. However, Catalyst (public charter schools) established roots in the Catholic Lasallian tradition not to defy law but to demonstrate that a public school can work well *within* the law as it embraces the vision and values of a Catholic saint and progressive educator, John Baptist de La Salle. This book explains how and why Catalyst Schools came into being, and explores the roadmap they provide for others inspired to follow their lead.

Catalyst Schools, a faith-inspired (not faith-based) two-campus charter school group serving grades K-12, was started in Chicago's North Lawndale through the dedication of a few Christian Brothers. The history of Catalyst is simple. The brothers wanted to venture into the public sector without compromising any of the values they brought from Catholic Lasallian schools and without overstepping the First Amendment. The Catalyst Schools intended to address the need of underserved children who could benefit from the 335-year-old Lasallian educational tradition of touching minds and especially touching hearts. It is a tradition in pursuit of both academic knowledge and values. Through core values of Hope, Rigor, Results, and Relationship, the Catalyst Schools brought the inspiration of John Baptist de La Salle to the public school system.

I believe the Lasallian mission is rooted within me not because I am employed by Catalyst, but rather by virtue of my upbringing as a follower of an Abrahamic religion—Islam. The values of human dignity, social justice, and emotional well-being are important to Islam. De La Salle's vision is about building bonds and creating fraternal, caring relationships and community with students. As Brother Mike Fehrenbach states in this book, "De La Salle was concerned with the journey into the depth of the human heart." To truly understand oneself, one must also adhere to the Golden Rule. In the Qur'an we hear, "They are all enjoined to observe the ties of kinship" (Q.4:1). De La Salle's vision is not incompatible with Islam.

Standing beside my Catalyst family is humbling. This community has inspired me to do better and to be better. I believe Catalyst is doing the work of God and living within constitutional bounds. At Catalyst, the expectation is to see your work as self-sacrificial and rooted in compassion for, and faith in, humanity and its potential for salvation. The teachers at Catalyst Schools, much like the brothers of Reims, come as "full human beings," authentic, and "not playing the role of the teacher." The school diligently assists teachers to achieve their full potential. Love, central to the Lasallian vision, is fostered and the result is zeal for each student's well-being.

Students are the heart of the organization. Everything is done for the betterment of their young minds and hearts, families and neighborhoods. Care and compassion for the underserved are at the heart of the Catalyst mission as inspired by Saint John Baptist de La Salle.

The mission of Catalyst Schools is much like this scripture from Qur'an: "Whoever saves the life of one human being, it shall be as if he had saved the whole of humankind" (5:32). At Catalyst Schools we emphasize saving humankind by serving each and every child who comes through our doors.

Introduction

"I know! I know!" Children respond enthusiastically at Catalyst Schools Circle Rock Campus.

Catholic schools in the United States can trace their beginnings to Florida in 1606, when Franciscan monks established a mission school among natives there. As the country developed, however, it was public schools that became most popular. Predominantly Protestant religious schools, they used the King James translation of the Bible as their primary religious text. According to one story, the first Catholic school in Boston was begun in 1859 in response to the beating of a young Catholic boy who would not read the Ten Commandments aloud from the King James Bible. True or not, the tale speaks of the religious divisions that existed and suggests motivation for a growing drive in the Catholic community to educate its own youth with the vision of the Church.

The Catholic school system began to develop with strength in the mid-nineteenth century. A century later, by the mid-1950s, nearly every Catholic child was assumed enrolled in a parish school, and these were supported by the almost free labor of the women religious who ran them. Schooling was a huge commitment of labor and resources by the Church. If a family was a supporting member of a parish, their children could attend the parish school at minimal cost. One of the most basic reasons parents sent their children to religious schools was to pass the religious culture from generation to generation. The religious nature of the schools, however, never minimized the importance of strong academics. Children who attended Catholic schools were well educated in secular as well as religious content and most of them, along with their public school counterparts, went on to significant success in life. Strong education was the backbone of progress and development for the country. Prosperity informed by strong values, whether learned within parochial systems like the Catholic schools or from the more Protestant-influenced public schools, greatly shaped the cultural development of the United States.

As society has become more diverse, including religiously diverse, educating for explicitly religious values has become increasingly controversial, and the effort to remove such values—or at least to refrain from identifying them as "religious" in public school settings—has been enshrined in law. The gulf between religious educational systems and the public schools has deepened as well.

Such a reality is neither useful nor good for children, however. Both public and religious school systems have deep value. That being the case, doesn't the welfare of children demand more collaboration and cooperation between the systems rather than intense competition? Furthermore, must the public sector fear religious values, or the religious community assume that public education is "value-free"? In fact, don't both systems share, teach, and practice many values? And shouldn't this be a cause for celebration?

Enter the Charter School Movement

The evolution of charter schools in the United States has the potential to reduce this anxiety—both public and parochial—over values. The charter school movement maintains neutrality about religion but not about values, part of its strong appeal to many families.

The growth of charter schools over the past fifteen years in many US cities is impressive.[1] These independently run public schools are intentionally more experimental, free (within limits) to establish policies, procedures, budgets, curricula, and hiring practices without the same level of bureaucratic control as the traditional public school. Part of the motivation for establishing such schools is, in fact, to develop and exercise new best practices with less bureaucratic interference. Accompanying this greater freedom, charters must comply with state regulations and are accountable for results. The charter can be revoked if either compliance or results do not meet minimal standards established by State Charter School Law.

In some ways, charter schools may offer a way to bridge the divide that exists between parochial and public educational systems—a bridge built on this intentionality and openness about values. No parent is obligated to send their child to a charter school and so the school must be deliberately chosen. Often, parents choose a charter school because of its values and the culture that arises from those values, as well as the academic results many judge these values to produce.

This book reflects on the experience of one charter school community that has intentionally tried to bridge the divide between religious and public education while answering a public desire for strong values-infused education. Catalyst Schools in Chicago, a two-campus charter school group serving grades K-12, grew out of the Catholic educational system, and specifically schools associated with the De La Salle Christian Brothers, a Catholic religious teaching community that has operated schools throughout the world since 1680. Popularly known as Lasallian schools, the name derives from the founder's name, John Baptist De La Salle, a seventeenth-century French priest.

The Controversy over Values

The simple fact is, children need to be educated and children need to develop a sense of coherent values that will guide their lives and help them become good, whole, well-integrated people. It is difficult to create the structure children need and crave in an institution that tries to be "values-free."

---

1. "Since 1999, the share of students in charter schools has grown from under 1 percent to over 5 percent. In the same time period, the number of charter schools has risen by almost 5,000. In contrast, the number of non-charter schools has increased by only 326 since the 1999-2000 school year. . . . Across the country, 2.5 million students attended 6,440 charter schools during the 2013–14 school year, according to data from the National Alliance for Public Charter Schools." Jason Russell, "Charter school movement is growing," *Washington Examiner,* May 7, 2015, http://www.washingtonexaminer.com/charter-school-movement-is-growing/article/2564134.

An educational system need not be "religious" in order to have and teach values. All educational systems have values. A claim of religious neutrality is itself a value statement. Public schools embrace and articulate a range of values and are operated by adults who likewise profess and live values. Values in this context are often articulated as rules for behavior (e.g., no bullying; dress appropriately; maintain decorum in the cafeteria; etc.), but they are not called values.

The founders of Catalyst Schools wanted to be clear about the values undergirding the culture of their schools. Catalyst, Chicago articulates those values as "Relationship," "Rigor," "Results," and "Hope."[2] Those values, in turn, reflect five core values that are part of the Lasallian tradition of education dating back to 1680. That tradition may be summarized as education that emphasizes and articulates values embraced by Lasallian education historically and worldwide, widely articulated as a Spirit of Faith, Living Gospel Values, Academic Excellence, Inclusive Community and Respect, and a Commitment to Justice and the Poor.[3] While these are values shared by Lasallian schools throughout the world, the Catalyst team believed they could be articulated as the foundation stones for a public school as well, without violating the US First Amendment prohibition that maintains the separation of church and state.

This book attempts to explain how Catalyst has made every effort to create such a values-centric public school, and to describe how such a school looks, acts, and believes. An additional hope is that describing the Catalyst philosophy and experience will be useful to other Lasallian educators who are interested in the public school option as a way of living their mission. Quite possibly, John Baptist de La Salle's experience and the evolution of the Lasallian schools during the last three centuries might hold some clues about some commonly held values we might all benefit from embracing.

Each of the five core Lasallian values will be explored in turn, both as the value evolved in the early Lasallian community and the experience of De La Salle, and also as it can apply within a public school today. The spirit of faith and the values of the Christian Gospel that inform the Lasallian tradition initially created roadblocks to conversation between the faith

---

2. "Our Values," the catalyst schools, http://www.catalystschools.org/about-us/our-value.

3. A comparison paralleling Catalyst Schools values and the Lasallian tradition of education might look like this, with Catalyst value(s) first and Lasallian values in parentheses: Relationship (inclusive community, respect, social justice), Hope (faith and Gospel values), Results and Rigor (academic excellence, quality education). The Lasallian preference for the poor is evidenced in the neighborhoods where Catalyst Schools are located and the population they serve (e.g., 95%–99% free and reduced lunch—these are high-poverty communities).

community and the public educational sector regarding the establishment of the Catalyst charter model. The ultimate success of this model, however, demonstrates that as other communities consider creating similarly modeled charters, there need be no such presumption of conflict.

A Uniquely American Point of View

> CONGRESS SHALL MAKE NO LAW *respecting an establishment of religion, or prohibiting the free exercise thereof; or abridging the freedom of speech, or of the press; or the right of the people peaceably to assemble, and to petition the Government for a redress of grievances.*
>
> ❦ **THE FIRST AMENDMENT TO THE U.S. CONSTITUTION**
> 15 DECEMBER 1791

© Anna Bryukhanova / iStock.com

Memorial plaque narrating the First Amendment in the US Constitution, Independence National Historical Park, Old City, Philadelphia.

The First Amendment to the US Constitution—and also the lesser-known yet highly influential Blaine Amendment, to be discussed in greater detail shortly—provide a useful starting point for this conversation. Popular agreement as well as legal standards support the principle that there should be no proselytizing or otherwise attempting to influence specific religious faith preferences in children by administrators or teachers in public schools. However, there are ways to articulate a rich faith *experience* that connects not to proselytizing or promoting doctrine or a specific faith tradition, but rather to practicing and teaching a set of values that provide a framework for a life well lived as productive and contributing citizens motivated to build a better society. The experiences offered at Catalyst Schools introduce students to these values by providing a deep context for humanizing education and children and building a flourishing community.

Before the colonial era, early immigration to the New World resulted, in part, from religious repression and persecution. Settlers left all that they knew—their culture, their families, their work, their lives—for a kind of freedom they could not experience in their homeland. The hardships of life in the New World were viewed as a small price to pay for the benefits received. The inspiration of freedom, the ability to be your own person, to have the opportunity to make it by the sweat of your brow, to raise your children as you saw fit—all gave rise to the great American dream that continues to be articulated in ways that guide the ongoing development of US culture in the twenty-first century.

More specifically, religious freedom has always been central to who we are as a culture. In fact, religious believers at war with each other in their homeland have learned to thrive side by side in the United States. The wisdom of the founding vision that protects religious freedom cannot be minimized. The First Amendment that prohibits government from establishing a religion and protects each person's right to practice (or not practice) any faith without government interference is unquestionably wise. All religious traditions in the United States enjoy this freedom and all should embrace and defend its cause.

Yet articulating and enforcing the First Amendment also has led to some historical miscues. One such misstep took shape in the form of the Blaine Amendment of 1875. Although the amendment ultimately failed at the federal level, some state interpretations and applications of the failed rule have created a certain trepidation regarding what appropriate and healthy involvement of the religious sector in the public educational sphere might be. Yet even these misunderstandings carry a silver lining, in that they force efforts such as the Catalyst Schools to a heightened and healthy intentionality and articulation of their mission, values, and practice. More on that to come, but first, a closer look at the Blaine Amendment.

The Blaine Amendment, December 14, 1875

"No State shall make any law respecting an establishment of religion or prohibiting the free exercise thereof; and no money raised by taxation in any State, for the support of public schools, or derived from any public fund therefor, nor any public lands devoted thereto, shall ever be under the control of any religious sect, nor shall any money so raised, or lands so devoted be divided between religious sects or denominations."[1]

> Rep. James G. Blaine (1830-1893) of Maine proposed [the Blaine Amendment to the US Constitution] on December 14, 1875 in reaction to efforts of, in particular, the Catholic Church to establish parochial schools. The amendment was passed by the House on August 4, 1876 by an overwhelming majority (180 votes in favor, 7 votes opposed), but failed to muster the necessary two-thirds vote in the Senate (28 votes in favor, 16 votes opposed). Afterwards, the Blaine Amendment was incorporated into a number of state constitutions, especially in the West, where its inclusion was often a prerequisite for consideration for statehood.
>
> Many First Amendment scholars consider the Blaine Amendment unconstitutional because it requires government to discriminate against religious groups.[2]
>
> More insulting is the fact the court had to invent the fiction of substantive due process in order to rewrite "Congress shall make no law" to "No State shall make no [sic] law" in order to apply to the States, something that never was successful through seven attempts to amend the Constitution post Fourteenth Amendment to make the Establishment Clause in some form or another applicable against the States.[3]

While the Blaine Amendment failed to garner sufficient support to become enshrined in the federal constitution, it has greatly influenced states throughout the country. States generally continue to live by the intent and letter of Blaine's intervention.

The negative mandate "no state shall make any law respecting an establishment of religion or prohibiting the free exercise thereof" becomes incredibly difficult to understand and implement in day-to-day life. When has a public employee (teacher, administrator, staff member) crossed the line and violated the law? Is wearing a religious symbol by a public employee allowed? Is sponsoring a student-led prayer group permitted? Is prayer be-

---

1. Text of the Federal Blaine Amendment.

2. "Blaine Amendment, December 14, 1875," The Religious Liberty Archive: A Service of the Religious Institutions Group, Lewis Roca Rothgerber, http://churchstatelaw.com/library/historical-materials/blaine-amendment-december-14-1875/.

3. P.A. Madison, "Misunderstanding Jefferson's 'wall of separation' metaphor," The Federalist Blog: Where Federalism is Kept Honest, http://www.federalistblog.us/2010/11/_defending_jeffersons_wall_of_separation_metaphor/.

fore a football game a violation of the establishment clause or is it the free exercise of religion by student athletes? What about a moment of silence in a classroom? Can we teach about religion and, if we can, should we? Can a teacher speak about her own beliefs or values? Is it okay to read the Bible in the faculty room?

Because new situations arise regularly, the separation of church and state as lived in the schools remains a controversial and frequently visited topic and often is resolved in the courts. Even what seems settled is not set in concrete, at least as far as the Anti-Defamation League is concerned.

> The issue of the proper role of religion in the public schools continues to be the subject of great controversy. School officials, parents and students—as well as lawyers and judges—wrestle with these questions every day. However, clear standards and guidance are elusive.[4]

So what is a school supposed to do?

> In practice, this means that the public schools must never endorse—or appear to endorse—any religion or religious practice. Indeed, not only may they not appear to endorse religion, but they may never appear to disapprove of religion either. Moreover, schools may not give the impression that they endorse religious belief over non-belief or any particular belief over others.
>
> The principle that public schools must never endorse or disapprove of religion has been established in a long line of US Supreme Court decisions. Students must never be given the impression that their school officially prefers or sanctions a particular religion or religion generally. Further, students must never feel coerced by pressure from their peers or from the public to adhere to any religion.[5]

This means the school must maintain neutrality toward all religions.

The employees of a charter school that purports to follow the inspiration of Saint John Baptist de La Salle in the United States must follow the same legal standard applied to any other public school employee—that is, to maintain neutrality toward all religions. It is neither permissible nor legal to promote Catholicism, Judaism, Islam, Buddhism, Christianity, or any other

---

4. "Religion in the Public Schools," Anti-Defamation League, http://www.adl.org/assets/pdf/civil-rights/religiousfreedom/rips/ReligPubSchs-PDF.pdf, 1.

5. Ibid., 4.

religious or spiritual "ism" or "anity." And subtle influence upon children regarding religious belief must be avoided.

What about Faith?

But does this mean there is no room in the world of public education for the values taught and lived in the private religious educational realm? Given the constitutional context in which "faith-inspired" charter schools are developing, how can they function and be true both to their foundational beliefs and the law? Is this an attempt to be true to two masters? Superficially, it seems that way. However when taking a deeper dive, possibly not.[6]

Saint John Baptist de La Salle believed the purpose of the Christian School was salvation. By this he meant the school was to teach a value system based on faith in God and acquisition of the life skills that made integration into and advancement in productive social citizenship possible. Today's public educational structures are concerned with the "salvation" of children as well, though they would understand this in the secular sense of economic and social success. If you watch daytime television, likely you will notice an abundance of advertisements for colleges that are skilled at promoting career advancement but rarely market themselves as institutions that encourage and support a balanced education or the development of the whole person. This attitude seems dominant in society at large as well. Many parents send their children to school so they can get a job and make money. The salvation De La Salle envisioned was about much more than that. He was concerned with the journey into the depth of the human heart.

In fact, progressive public and private/religious educational systems are not fundamentally at odds. Those working in them want the same thing for children and society. The goals remain the well-being ("saving") of children and that they grow into whole, healthy, productive, contributing members of society. Achievement of this outcome requires that we give them a value system that helps them establish a moral compass and can form the basis of healthy relationships. Teach them the Golden Rule. Provide a vision of community that says my ego is not the only thing that matters in the world. Give them the requisite skills for life in a twenty-first century that experiences change so rapidly that predictions about the future children will be living in are tenuous at best.

---

6. An excellent guide to help a school maintain appropriate boundaries is the resource: "Know Your Rights: Religion in Public Schools: A Guide for Administrators and Teachers," http://www.aclu-tn.org/pdfs/briefer_religion_in_public_schools.pdf.

Students listen during a career day presentation at Catalyst Circle Rock.

2 Culture

Catalyst Schools and the Lasallian tradition in education emphasize a strong commitment to justice, quality education, a style of teaching, the benefit of positive and healthy relationships between caring adults and children, and a context of faith in which these things happen.

The culture of any organization is the glue that holds it together. A culture is the way of life of a group of people—the behaviors, beliefs, values, and symbols that they accept, generally without thinking about them, and that are passed along by communication and imitation from one generation to the next.

Culture may be the most important element in the life of a corporate enterprise and, while less tangible, has deeper value than product, structure, or bottom line. All of these things depend on the successful development, evolution, and living of the culture that becomes the identity of a community. Families have a culture. Cities have a culture. Nations have a culture. Most of the time, people aren't thinking about their culture because culture is to human beings like water is to fish. A story retold by David Foster Wallace illustrates this well.

> There are these two young fish swimming along and they happen to meet an older fish swimming the other way, who nods at them and says, "Morning, boys. How's the water?" And the two young fish swim on for a bit, and then eventually one of them looks over at the other and goes, "What the hell is water?"[1]

Culture is like the air we breathe, the atmosphere we walk through each day. It is so central that we don't look at it, don't see it, and don't experience it as something separate from our very selves. Yet, it holds our lives together. It is, in significant ways, what makes us who we are.

Culture is so important that Deal and Peterson, in *Shaping School Culture*, say "the culture of an enterprise plays the dominant role in exemplary performance."[2] They go on to say that anything can become reality when people put their whole heart into making it so. Heart is central to culture. Culture grows from within and is not imposed from the outside. This is why it is so important, in Saint John Baptist de La Salle's words, to "win hearts." The culture in a Lasallian school is a union of hearts around a common enterprise—the salvation of youth.

Howard Schulz, CEO of Starbucks, understands this truth about culture and heart. "A company can grow big without losing the passion and personality that built it, but only if it is driven not by profits but by values and people. . . . The key is heart. . . . When customers sense that, they respond in kind."[3]

When business leaders understand the nature of their corporate culture in this way, how much more so should the leaders of an institution whose purpose is transformation, such as a school. The culture of a school must first of all be driven by a leader who is servant to the community. Robert Greenleaf, in *The Servant as Leader*, expresses this well.

---

1. David Foster Wallace, "This Is Water," 2005 Kenyon College Commencement Address (delivered May 21, 2005), http://web.ics.purdue.edu/~drkelly/DFWKenyonAddress2005.pdf.

2. Terrence E. Deal and Kent D. Peterson, *Shaping School Culture: The Heart of Leadership* (San Francisco: Jossey-Bass Publishers, 1999), 1.

3. Ibid.

The difference manifests itself in the care taken by the servant—first to make sure that other people's highest priority needs are being served. The best test, and difficult to administer, is: Do those served grow as persons? Do they, while being served, become healthier, wiser, freer, more autonomous, more likely themselves to become servants? And, what is the effect on the least privileged in society? Will they benefit or at least not be further deprived?

A servant-leader focuses primarily on the growth and well-being of people and the communities to which they belong. While traditional leadership generally involves the accumulation and exercise of power by one at the "top of the pyramid," servant leadership is different. The servant-leader shares power, puts the needs of others first and helps people develop and perform as highly as possible.[4]

The "soft" side of schools, the more intangible, ephemeral dimensions, are frequently ignored when discussing growth, improvement, and achievement. But these are the things that are at the essence of culture. A discipline code should not create culture. A curriculum should not create culture. Discipline codes, curriculum, and such are most appropriate and effective when they grow out of culture—the beliefs, values, and symbols held in common by the community. Codes, curriculum, policies, and routines should not create the value basis of the school but rather ought to reflect the deeply embedded values that grow from within the community.

When embarking on the creation of a "faith-inspired" school (one that grows out of a faith community but is not dedicated to spreading or proselytizing that community's doctrinal propositions), it is critical to keep the culture of the organization in mind. Culture grows in relationship before it emerges in structure. Building community is how we build culture, and how we build culture will determine the kind of school we have.

Cultural Challenge for a Faith-Inspired Public School

When the Catalyst founders decided to begin a "faith-inspired" charter school, legal counsel advised that any violation of the prohibition against "mixing" church with state would land in court and be the end of the work they were trying to do. Every attempt was made to be cautious and to live specific spiritual values within the boundaries set forth in law. There has

---

4. Robert K. Greenleaf, *The Servant as Leader* (Atlanta: The Greenleaf Center for Servant Leadership, rev. ed. 2015), 6.

been no evangelizing and no proselytizing at the Catalyst Schools. In fact, some have accused Catalyst of being too cautious. Although Catalyst has never been taken to court and no one has accused it of violating the law, the leadership in fact may have been overly fearful about these things. For example, words such as *faith*, *Christian*, and certainly *Catholic* have been carefully avoided. Professional development promoted good teaching but never mentioned the spiritual context of the mission. Fear, engendered by legal counsel, about the possibility of being sued led to cautious and almost scrupulous risk avoidance behavior that confused staff. We spoke the language of mission and value but acted as though those ideas were subservient to law rather

© John Lee, John Lee Pictures ht.

A boy enjoys some quiet reading time at Catalyst Schools Circle Rock Campus.

than demonstrating that law and values are not contradictory in practice. It was not until the schools had been operating for two years that leadership began to figure out they could be more direct regarding the tradition out of which the schools were founded. The fact is, no one knew of any other group that had tried to take the values underlying a private, faith-based educational system into the public school sector.

Because of this lack of precedent, none of the organizers knew how, or if, this could work. While there was no blueprint for creating such a school, there was the belief that if this new model functioned as hoped, it could bring a wonderful gift to the general public and become an asset in the education of the whole child. For example, Catalyst Schools set out to establish a system of discipline that would be a learning experience rather than a system of punishments, and to help close the achievement gap for minority students in many neighborhoods where Catholic schools had had to close.

Catalyst Schools is an effort to bring back to public education something that changed in its evolution from its Protestant roots. Historically public schools, along with Catholic schools, helped create a strong middle class educated in content areas, and delivered that education in the context of a cohesive values system that anchored the culture. In an effort to value and protect diversity, however, what of this values context has been lost? Have we abandoned common sense in embracing diversity? Did acknowledging the fact that life is plural, not singular, mean there are no commonly held values that shape our culture and our world? There may not be many, but aren't there any?

Cultural Contribution of John Baptist de La Salle

John Baptist de La Salle was a Roman Catholic priest who lived and worked in France at the end of the seventeenth and beginning of the eighteenth centuries. Society at that time was rigidly constructed around social class, and the wealthy benefited from advantages the poor could never dream of embracing. De La Salle was a member of the upper class. His mother was a Moet and we still drink the family's champagne today. While there are many differences between seventeenth-century France and twenty-first-century United States, we have things in common beyond champagne.

For example, the poor are still with us. Though we do not have the estates that grounded life in De La Salle's France, our culture is built upon its own class structure, and the gap between rich and poor grows increasingly wider. No different than in De La Salle's time, children continue to have babies, use drugs, run the streets, join gangs, and otherwise live without appropriate adult supervision. Children are being lost, and our cities, states, and country

Saint John Baptist de La Salle

are the poorer because the wealth of talent these children possess is being squandered.

To demonstrate his faith in God, De La Salle gave his wealth to the poor and hungry during a ravaging famine and otherwise tried to respond to conditions enslaving the poor children of his time. These children roamed the streets unsupervised, dirty, hungry, lost, and destined to remain the marginalized of society, an underclass whose talent would be thrown to the wind and scattered like dust. De La Salle began the Christian Schools and trained teachers to be effective in working with these throwaway kids. He believed it was faith and a life rooted in God, combined with strong academic training, that would make the difference. His schools were designed to provide children with excellent, faith-filled teachers who embraced their students in a positive and healthy relationship. De La Salle's Christian Schools offered these scholars the opportunity to acquire life skills and spiritual balance.

De La Salle was frequently misunderstood by the religious hierarchy and the educational system of his day. Against all obstacles put in his path by his own Catholic Church and the teacher unions, such as they were at the time, he developed a thriving network of schools that gave the poor and the ignorant an education that helped them integrate into and advance through society while maintaining a deep sense of value. These throwaway children were given the chance to become whole, healthy, productive people. De La

Salle's success can be seen in the fact that even in his day, his teachers and schools were requested throughout France. His network grew throughout the world and continues today, nearly 300 years after his death in 1719.

In the United States we live with the prohibition against crossing church/state boundaries. Employees of government agencies such as public schools, as well as public funds (taxes), may not promote or inhibit religious expression. This means that in public schools it is not possible to teach religion, offer religious exercises, preach, evangelize, or proselytize. One also may not inhibit such activity provided it is organized, implemented, or promoted by the students or their parents, and the activity is not disruptive of other students' rights. In sum, public schools must remain neutral in religious matters.

So how can a public school claim a Lasallian identity and culture when Lasallian schools were clearly founded in part to be explicit proclaimers of the Gospel of Jesus Christ? How can there be such a thing as a public school founded upon the Lasallian tradition?

We Construct the Reality We Live

Peter Berger speaks about the "social construction of reality." Through human interaction in social community we generate a language and perception of the "way things are" and can be said to create the ethos or reality in which we live. An example of this "social creation" is offered by A.J. Henderson.

> Social construction of reality refers to an idea that reality is based on what the majority of people or society believes. For example, in the US, the social construction of reality surrounding the events of September 11th 2001 is that terrorists attacked the American people in a horrific attack. This resulted in our just war against the Taliban. However, in an Al Queda training camp, the reality would be that brave "heroes" took control of a plane of the evil Americans and attacked the structure of the government that oppresses them. Then, America turned the world against them and destroyed their just cause.[5]

This dramatic example offers a glimpse into how a community shapes and lives its particular vision of what matters, of the way things are, of the reality we come to believe and value; such a vision provides the foundation out of

---

5. A.J. Henderson, "Social Construction of Reality," https://ajhenderson.com/pdf/Social%20Construction%20of%20Reality.pdf. See also Peter Berger and Thomas Luckmann, *The Social Construction of Reality: A Treatise in the Sociology of Knowledge* (Random House: New York, 1966), for a full discussion of their ideas.

which we live our daily lives, individually and corporately. Our identity and our behavior emerge from the commonly held belief about reality in which we are immersed.

The "Lasallian Way" has been constructed through community interaction, a network of personal and professional relationships, and an articulated vision rising out of lived experience over the course of the past three centuries, beginning in 1680 as an officially recognized start of the Lasallian enterprise.

Educators in Lasallian schools throughout the world have integrated a set of values into their most important work. Although there are variations in how the values are articulated (see also footnote 3 in the introduction to this book), it is possible to recognize a Lasallian school just by being present in one. They have a strong commitment to justice, a shared language and vocabulary about quality education, a style of teaching, a belief about the potential benefit of positive and healthy relationships between compassionate and caring adults and children, and a context of faith in which these things happen.

This way of being, this Lasallian approach, has been communicated through ongoing lived relationships, formation in community, the transference of ideas through instruction, conferences, collaborative sharing of ideas and ideals, and in former days, through the living together in a religious community known as the Brothers of the Christian Schools, now more commonly known as the De La Salle Christian Brothers. Community members, in turn, were surrounded by the images, language, belief systems, and innovations that supported and sustained the created reality.

These brothers were the teachers in the Christian Schools founded by John Baptist de La Salle. The goal of the schools was the physical as well as the spiritual salvation of the young children roaming the streets of France.

Reality as Constructed in the Early Christian Schools—Mission

As has been noted, the mission of the first schools established by De La Salle was the salvation of youth. The culture of the schools ensured salvation of the young would be the focus of everything that was done. Salvation meant two fundamental things for the teachers in the Christian Schools.

First, give these young vagabonds the necessary skills to live a productive life. Reading and math were no less important in De La Salle's time than they are today. In addition handwriting (penmanship) was a critical skill—the seventeenth through the nineteenth centuries had no inkling of a digital age. Accountants, scribes, and many other occupations required knowledge of these three Rs. Education was practical. It had a quantifiable outcome beyond life in the school, and that was an occupation. That meant a young man (De La Salle's schools were for young boys) matriculating from a La-sallian school would be able to take care of himself and his family, shielding them from the elements and hunger. The practical goal of the school kept the long-term success of the student in mind. Whenever the need and there-fore the opportunity arose to help the young develop practical skills, the Lasallian brothers jumped on it. Why else would they train navigators, open boarding schools, work with juvenile delinquents, and more?

Schools were for young people and for their life in society. The curricu-lum of the school was designed to serve them. In his discussion of the Con-duct of Schools, Brother Leon Lauraire notes the organization of content that helped students advance on the basis of mastery.

> All these indications reveal a finely tuned system of graded attain-ment and a clear idea of a pupil's programme of studies. Each of the "orders" (levels of attainment) corresponded to a specific part of the programme, constituting a kind of concrete operational objective. It is useful to know that an order normally lasted a month, but could be repeated, following a monthly test, if the objectives had not been sufficiently mastered.[6]

Second and most importantly in the mission of the Christian Schools was the communication of the faith that grounded the worldview of Western Europe, and France in particular, during the time the Christian Schools took root there. The brothers were men of faith and evangelization was essential to their mission. It was imperative to help the young understand the human and Christian values that were central to the Christian Gospel. In this way, not only were they prepared to live a life, they were equipped with a moral compass that motivated them to adopt the most fundamental value of all—treat others as you want to be treated. The Christian Schools were built upon relationship. Brother Lauraire emphasizes this point.

> John Baptist de La Salle and the Brothers were convinced that the most important aspect of education depended on the quality of the relationship between teacher and pupil. On numerous occasions, De La Salle insists in his writings on the need to create strong and warm relationships in school. In particular, as we have seen, he exhorts the Brothers "to win over hearts."[7]

6. Brother Leon Lauraire, "The *Conduct of Schools*: Pedagogical Approach," *Cahiers Lasal-liens* 62 (Rome, 2006), 46.

7. Ibid., 177.

Empathy, compassion, and love were the foundation stones for the network of valued relationships that would sustain a person throughout life. It was not enough to be a competent wage earner. It was equally important to be a good and moral person.

Today's Emerging Realities

While the salvation of youth remains the focus of all genuine Lasallian educational endeavors, in the United States, those endeavors are no longer centralized in the community of De La Salle Christian Brothers. Today thousands of men and women educators have embraced the vision, philosophy, and spirituality of Saint John Baptist De La Salle, thus expanding the socially conceived notion that only an institutionalized religious community can hold the gift (charism) that this vision and mission are for the world. It is a gift, and the giver offers it to whomever. Many have been called to embrace the vision and live the spirit of the Lasallian worldview.

Currently, in the United States, more than 3,000 educators claim a connection to the Lasallian mission. Fewer than one third of these are the traditional Christian Brother.

Forging new paths, new venues, and new approaches to serve the poor and disenfranchised is not new in the Lasallian world. While the inspiration and core mission have remained the essential foundation of the schools, adaptation of the strategies for implementation has always been the experience. Creativity is part of the heritage because change is inevitable.

When De La Salle died, Christian Brothers in France worried what might become of their vulnerable community of fewer than one hundred members. Later, when they were dispersed due to the French Revolution and more dramatically after the 1904 legislation that made it illegal for religious to teach, it seemed like their demise. However, it was really the birth of an international reality not envisioned at the beginning. The small bands of brothers took root wherever they landed.

The fact that we continue to discover new pathways to save youth and the fact that educators implement the mission in ways not previously foreseen are consistent with how Lasallian educators have always behaved. The gift continues to be given because the need is so great—throughout the world and definitely no less in the United States. De La Salle did not start a school but, according to Brother Gerard Rummery, launched a movement, in the sense that in every situation there was a kind of refounding and a new application of enduring principles.

There is a profound sense in which every new opening since the first school in Saint-Maurice in 1679 has been a refoundation because the same underlying principles of the Lasallian heritage have led to its creation. Among these principles one would have to include the following four:

- the foundation is a response in the spirit of the Gospel to the particular needs of those to be served;
- those responsible for the work are associated together in what they see as a common enterprise and are prepared to work together to achieve its ends;
- the basis of relationships, among those who serve as well as among those being served, is that of being "brothers/sisters to one another and older brothers/sisters to those served";
- a profound sense of gratuity, material and spiritual, characterizes the policies of the foundation.[8]

© Mike Fehrenbach, FSC

Catalyst staff enjoy canoeing together while on retreat. Currently, in the United States, more than 3,000 educators claim a connection to the Lasallian mission. Fewer than one third of these are the traditional Christian Brother.

---

8. Gerard Rummery, FSC, "The Journey of the Lasallian Community," *Lasallian Identity: Five Documents for a Workshop*, Secretariat for Lasallian Associates (2004), 13.

In the Midst of Change,
the Poor Remain Central to the Vision

The first Christian (Lasallian) Schools were always gratuitous. Although founded to have a special preference for the poor, no one was ever turned away. Rich and poor alike, the gifted and the most challenged, were welcome. It was an inclusive community that bridged social class and academic ability. No one paid in these early schools. All shared the same rich blessing of education.

De La Salle was not only the inspirational axis for this foundation, he was also the Servant Leader who guided, nurtured, cared for, and responded to need. In addition he worked for the financial sustenance of the schools. He was a founder who first organized a group of teachers and taught them to establish and run excellent schools. He was an animator whose religious vision was central to the community his teachers eventually became. He was the leader who knew his teachers, knew their schools, knew the children and the context of their lives. He listened, coached, mentored, and gave professional and personal guidance to his brothers. He was also fundraiser, networking with supporters like Madame de Maillefer, who was generous in her support of schools for poor girls and later for poor boys.[9] Later, De La Salle also opened boarding schools that educated students whose families could pay. These schools helped support the gratuitous schools.

In the United States, over time, private education has become so expensive the once thriving private school systems have increasingly become largely a benefit only to those who can afford them. Tuition has been a necessity and the very poor for whom the Christian Schools were founded have often been priced out of them. Private and religious schools in economically challenged communities have been shuttering their schools at an alarming rate. Given these contemporary realities, the founders of Catalyst wanted to find another way to implement the Lasallian mission.

Return to the Question

How can the vision of a Catholic priest that emerged in seventeenth-century France become part of the reality of public education in the twenty-first-century United States?

This was the question the Catalyst Schools set out to explore in 2005 when the first proposal for a charter school was written. The first Catalyst

---

9. Luke Salm, FSC, *The Work Is Yours: The Life of St. John Baptist de La Salle* (Washington, DC: Christian Brothers Publications, 1996), 30.

School was opened in 2006 in the North Lawndale neighborhood of Chicago's largely impoverished African American west-side community. The second was opened in 2007 in the Austin neighborhood, also on Chicago's west side and also dealing with the challenges of economic poverty. The third was opened in 2012 in Chicago Lawn, a community composed of Latinos and African Americans and again, dealing with economic challenges. All three communities are confronted by gang activity, violence, and home foreclosure, all are food deserts, and all bear other stereotypical consequences of poverty. What is often missed are the incredible assets that keep these communities alive and thriving against all odds: strong family ties, strong faith, community organizations that breed hope, love of their children, a moral compass, the ability to suffer even when the suffering is imposed from without, belief in the American Dream in spite of how it's been withheld, witnessing small incremental change and being committed to a future that is better than the present. A common response to the question "How are you?" is "I'm blessed." While "I'm blessed" may be just a quick response like "Oh, I'm fine," it might also say volumes about the depth of these communities in which spiritual heritage is important. After all, the affirmation "I'm blessed" comes straight from the Beatitudes.[10]

Catalyst embraces the "socially constructed" view, consistent with Lasallian values, that the work of education is inspired by faith, that the values emerging from the Gospel are valid, that academic excellence is critically important, that community makes the entire system work, and that the school is a work of justice. These five values, taken together, offer the salvation that the young desperately needed when the Christian Schools first originated; they continue to offer that salvation today.

A genuinely Lasallian school is first and foremost one that is rooted in faith and that proclaims Gospel values. It always offers an excellent education. It is an educational enterprise built on the ideals of inclusive and collaborative community and respect for all persons—students, family members, teachers, staff, board members, and administrators. At its core is a passion for justice that demonstrates, in very practical ways, a special preference for the economically poor. All five of these values, or characteristics, are essential, and without any one of them, the Lasallian nature of the school is weakened.

This small but growing network of charter schools—Catalyst—remains true to the spirit of the five core values. Doing so, it enriches the lives of

---

10. Dave Johnson, July 2, 2015, "I'm not lucky, I'm . . . blessed?" *The Book of Fellows [GEN] ERATION TRANSFORMATION,* https://thebookoffellows.wordpress.com/2015/07/02/im-not-lucky-im-blessed/.

the students and families who enroll as well as the entire education system throughout Illinois and the United States. Saint John Baptist de La Salle lives in the works that have been inspired by his seminal vision. He continues to animate the motivations and the dreams of his followers.

And so, how can these core values be shaped so they remain authentic and still inform a system that requires the separation of church and state? We turn to that question now.

3

Core Lasallian Values

Saint John Baptist de La Salle

What are called *core values* here are articulated in diverse ways throughout the world because the Lasallian network of schools spans more than eighty countries and even more cultural contexts. However, these five values (Faith and Spirituality, Commitment to Gospel Values, Academic Excellence, Inclusive Community and Respect, Preferential Concern for the Poor and Justice)[1] are not unique experiences but are shared throughout the Lasallian educational systems. They derive from the life experience of De La

---

1. "5 Core Principles" (adapted from Brother Terry Collins), Brothers of the Christian Schools: Lasallian Region of North America, https://www.lasallian.info/lasallian-family/5-core-principles/.

Salle and the early experience of the first teachers gathered and trained by John Baptist de La Salle himself.

The early Christian Schools were dedicated to service of the poor youth roaming the streets of Rheims, France. De La Salle knew that one of the key elements needed to end poverty and to turn street kids into productive, caring citizens was education. But it wasn't just any education and especially not the kind generally available in France at the time. It would be an education grounded in a strong academic program that was infused with and inspired by a deep commitment to mission and the values expressed in his reading of the Gospel. If children were to grow into adults who could care for themselves and for others, both of these elements had to be present and fully integrated. Values infused the entire educational process, the schools' academic programs, and the relationships that made each school work.

De La Salle believed the education of these poor boys could be best served by a community of adults who demonstrated in their own lives and relationships—with one another and their students—that the future faced by these children could be better than the circumstances in which they currently lived. The school was to make real, in the present moment, the dream of a better world. For De La Salle, salvation was not limited to some distant future reality but was a here-and-now experience for children who were hungry, unsupervised, without skills or self-discipline, and many without a caring presence in their lives.

The reflection that follows attempts to articulate, for our own time, the core values that made De La Salle's schools so successful that they eventually took root in eighty countries around the globe. In addition, this reflection attempts to demonstrate how these values can be applicable today, in the United States, and in a public school system where the separation of church and state must be maintained. No doubt this separation provides, in itself, a strong value and attempts to enshrine respect for all belief systems by not endorsing any one. This value has much merit and should be upheld and embraced. Respect is, of course, one of the core values of the Lasallian philosophy of education.

Of the five values to be discussed, two—faith and Gospel values—at first blush may seem quite inappropriate to a public school setting. Yet, conceived as dynamic experiences and action rather than doctrine, these values may be seen as already present in much of our public education. Nor is it a stretch to see how these two core values can become foundation stones in the public system of education. While the state cannot establish or promote any religion, the values inherent in faith and the Christian Gospel go beyond doctrine and any particular religious or spiritual tradition. They are in fact central to what it means to be human—viewed anthropologically and not from a religious perspective at all.

There is likely little debate about the other three core values (Academic Excellence, Inclusive Community and Respect, and Concern for the Poor and Justice) as desirable foundation stones for an educational system in the public arena, since a strong case can be made for them regardless of religion even though many of the concepts they entail originate in the sacred texts of various faiths.

All five values ought to be judged on their meaning, however, not their source. In other words, what does each value intend? If we proceed from that question, a productive conversation can ensue. These five core values are embedded in the Lasallian tradition, and they have probably influenced the public educational enterprise for centuries. The Lasallian schools attempt to be explicit in articulating and embracing them, however. These five values give direction and substance to all Lasallian schools. Properly understood and expressed, they can give direction and substance to a public charter school as well.

Core Value: Faith and Spirituality

The issue of faith is central to any discussion of an attempt to create a public school in the Lasallian tradition. For De La Salle faith was about a relationship with God through the message and person of Jesus. His great desire was to be united to the wonderful mystery of God and his point of entry was the Christian Gospel.

De La Salle was raised in a large family committed to their Catholic faith. France was a Catholic nation. For him, it was important to introduce students to the basic principles of faith, which meant not only the doctrine of the Church but also a relationship with Jesus. He was a priest who was fully committed to the Church even when that very Church seemed incapable of responding in fidelity to him. Many of his battles in establishing the first schools were with ecclesiastics who could not understand his motivation and intent. To them, De La Salle seemed irresponsible by involving himself in such a non-church activity as running schools for indigent boys. The power and prestige of the national church would not be reflected in this work, they reasoned.

When De La Salle talked about faith as an essential component of salvation, however, triumphal imagery never colored his language. He always spoke of the love of Christ for his followers. He always spoke in images that took his companions and his students to the relational nature of the mystery that faith is. De La Salle spoke of the motherhood and fatherhood of God; of Christ the Good Shepherd who had a special relationship with his sheep;

of being ambassadors of good news and apostles who work tirelessly for the salvation of others. For him the experience of faith was one of relationship, and introducing children to the mysteries of life deeply significant.

De La Salle saw living and sharing the mystery of faith as a critical part of the educational process and created all kinds of methods for providing entry points for his teachers and students to walk into that mystery.

Faith in the Presence of God

Faith is most commonly associated with belief—a belief in God. It is also frequently associated with a system of doctrines that attempt to define it. People of faith often hold strong convictions about their system of belief. It's how we got the Reformation, the Counter-Reformation, the multitude of denominations and splinter groups within them. Especially if mixed with politics, faith may even lead to violence—for example, the Crusades or the attacks of 9–11. Often religious belief is inanimate, however. We may believe and go to a church on Sunday, a synagogue on Saturday, or participate in prayer each day at the mosque—and then simply go about our business.

Real faith, however, is something more than belief or doctrine or ritual. Faith is—or certainly should be—an experience that captures us, surrounds us, seduces us, gives us new ears and opens our eyes so we see life in new and unique ways. Real faith is dynamic not static. Faith isn't a noun but a verb.

In the preface to his book, *God Is a Verb,* Rabbi David Cooper says, "Our yearning to reconnect to our essential nature transcends the limits of the intellect. It comes from a place of inner knowing that there is far more to life than material wealth. We know deeply within that the mysteries of creation speak in a language that can only be absorbed through being."[2]

David Brooks, in an address delivered to the KIPP Charter School Network, elaborated on Rabbi Cooper's concept of "inner knowing" and that life is more than material. Brooks spoke of five experiences that we might consider a preparation for and entry into the world beyond the material— five experiences that we might possibly call a preparation for an experience of faith.[3]

Brooks contends that many people spend much of life, and some spend all of it, building a persona for the external world. For those fortunate enough to be able to make certain choices, such as about what career to

---

2. Rabbi David Cooper, *God Is a Verb: Kabbalah and the Practice of Mystical Judaism* (New York: Riverhead Books, The Berkeley Publishing Group, Penguin Putnam, 1998), viii.

3. David Brooks, "A Conversation on Character" (address to the KIPP Charter School Network, 2014), https://vimeo.com/103539021.

choose, where to live, what clothes to wear, and a host of other things, these are really choices about how one wants to project oneself to the rest of the world. Sometimes, parents choose or direct a career path for their children based on pay or prestige. Some people choose relationships because of the perceived "value add" they bring. In young adulthood, some people commit themselves to being successful as defined by a certain kind of economic logic. A person may be governed by Wall Street and Madison Avenue values as conveyed through advertising. Everyone has a degree of susceptibility to this kind of manipulation.

Although much of this superficiality and ego-construction constitutes normal (and particularly early) development, according to Brooks, it is fundamentally rooted in the superficial and things that are temporary and passing. No one takes their car, their home, their work with them when they go. Not only that, success built solely on the temporal realm can create distortions and illusions that may lead to a certain smugness about "having arrived." Observe how our contemporary society is built on work, production, staying busy, noise, speed, and so-called multi-tasking. Yet the old adage holds true: on their death bed, no one says, "I wish I had spent more time at the office."

So where are schools in all of this? Schools teach scholars how to develop a sense of grit and self-control, qualities which may lead students to the experience of immediate success. STEM (Science-Technology-Engineering-Math) is the critical curriculum now because we are in a race with other cultures for position and these fields have created what is largely viewed as the latest jobs frontier. This projection, in turn, generates a system intended to maintain our economic way of life. Such traits as "grit" and "resilience" are promoted as the essential qualities of successful students. These character traits, in fact, do lead to some immediate success and are indeed important. Explicitly religious or faith-inspired schools, however, have to be about more than immediate success and gratification. Likewise school discipline structures predicated solely on a system of reward and punishment reinforce lower-level moral thinking. Discipline codes need to teach an internal discipline built on critical thinking and analysis, empathy and an understanding of the common good.

Catalyst Schools, formed in the Lasallian tradition, recognize that the task at hand is to form the young in what Brooks describes as moral traits as well as performance traits. We adults, rooted in our own experience of deep values and faith commitments, must lead the young to long-term virtuous behavior that includes a commitment to seeking truth and the service of others.

Unlike that phase of life that imbues us with economic and marketplace values, this long-term virtuous path is about the inward journey, the exploration of the internal world—the spiritual journey. It is about who we are at our core; who we are when no one is looking. Who is that person staring back at us in the mirror when we are brutally honest with ourselves?

Brooks calls such moral values or moral traits "Eulogy Virtues." These are the values, the virtues that must guide the inward, the spiritual journey. The inward journey is about the kind of person we are, the nature of our relationships. It is what we hope is the deeper legacy we leave our children, our families, and our society. These are the virtues that matter most to the health of the world. The Catalyst Schools' community of adult educators is not only about academic excellence but about spiritual development, the internal journey toward authentic self of those entrusted to our care. We ask students to explore not only the external world but also their internal world.

The inward journey calls us to a profound sense of self. We experience life as a gradual discovery of who we are as persons, not performers or actors in the public, day-to-day workforce. The journey inward is concerned with bringing unity to our life—bringing all the pieces together into a coherent and cohesive whole.

While the virtues of the marketplace, when they become our primary values, often lead to a superficial life and a sense of self-importance, the deeper inward journey can lead to humility because we must embrace our failure—and there will be failure. The old spiritual maxim turns out to be true: It is in losing ourselves that we ultimately find ourselves. "For whoever wishes to save his life will lose it, but whoever loses his life for my sake will find it. What profit would there be for one to gain the whole world and forfeit his life? Or what can one give in exchange for his life?" (Matthew 16:25–26).

Or in more secular terms, "We travel, initially, to lose ourselves, and we travel, next, to find ourselves. We travel to open our hearts and eyes. . . . And we travel, in essence, to become young fools again—to slow time down and get taken in, and fall in love once more."[4] The journey toward self, the self who makes a real difference in the world, is about depth and not about "stuff."

Brooks asks: "What makes us a deeper person? How do we help our students prepare for the deeper journey and moral drama that is essential to reach a place of deep and abiding peace and spiritual well-being?" He answers that we must help students—and one another—embrace and appreciate five experiences. A paraphrase of Brooks' explanation follows.

1. Love: This is a grand and glorious gift. Sometimes we miss the gift even when it is explicitly presented because our culture is so filled with superficial

---

4. Pico Iyer, as found at http://www.goodreads.com/quotes/351425-we-travel-initially-to-lose-ourselves-and-we-travel-next.

and physical notions of love. We aren't talking about soap opera love, or simply about a feel-good experience. Love, as Brooks describes it, is significantly more challenging and a deep heart experience. Love is an experience of losing self. It is in love that we find we are not in control of life. As Brooks says, love decenters us because we discover our treasure is beyond us. The experience of love teaches us the truth that it is in giving that we receive.

Through the experience of loving, Saint Augustine tells us, the heart is enlarged. "The widening of the heart is the delight we take in righteousness. This is the gift of God, the effect of which is, that we are not straitened in His commandments through the fear of punishment, but widened through love, and the delight we have in righteousness" (Exposition on the Psalms).

Augustine gives more concrete admonition about love when he says: "What does love look like? It has the hands to help others. It has the feet to hasten to the poor and needy. It has eyes to see misery and want. It has the ears to hear the sighs and sorrows of men. That is what love looks like." This insight comes from a man who was truly lost for a while in pursuit of personal pleasure and self-gratification.

The Roman writer, statesman, and monk Cassiodorus reinforces Augustine's position: "They could not have either walked or run if their hearts had not been extended by breadth of knowledge, for though we read that the way of the commandments is narrow, we can run it only with heart enlarged. When the soul receives the light of truth, it is opened to recognitions of many kinds; it is broadened by knowledge of virtues after earlier being narrowed by sins."[5]

> "Where there is love there is life." (Mahatma Gandhi)

Love multiplies and grows and so does our capacity for love. Love is an inclusive experience, not an isolating one. But the truth as stated by Augustine and Cassiodorus explores love more deeply—it is first in failure, in falling and our honest recognition of it, our owning it, that we learn the power of empathy, of acceptance, of forgiveness, of the gift that life is. Through love our hearts are truly broken open and we gain the capacity for deeper relationship and deeper commitment. Love takes us beyond fear. Love takes us to knowledge. Love takes us to union and not separation.

For these reasons, the relationship between teacher and student must be genuine and authentic. The adult is, in De La Salle's words, the "Guardian Angel" in the child's life. The metaphor is clear. The teacher is a manifestation of love for the child as one who cares for, protects, and watches out

---

5. As found at http://psallamdomino.blogspot.com/2012/03/psalm-118-119-verse-32-en-large-my-heart.html.

for the child's well-being. The relationship demonstrates that love is more than what we see portrayed on television or in the movies. Entering a Catalyst School's kindergarten or first-grade classroom, one witnesses this in action. Because the teacher manages the classroom well, gives the children individualized attention, protects them from harm in the classroom and on the playground, and persists in holding high expectations, the children are relaxed and themselves. The trust built between teacher and student invites the children's hugs and greetings. Appropriate love creates for them a home away from home, a second family that nourishes them with more than food.

> *"Love is not affectionate feeling, but a steady wish for the loved person's ultimate good as far as it can be obtained."* (C.S. Lewis)

Positive teacher-student relationships are a priority at Catalyst Schools. Here a teacher assists a student at Catalyst Schools Circle Rock Charter.

2. Suffering: We learn incredible lessons in times of difficulty. Again, suffering tells us that we are not in control. We are not in charge. Life, authentically lived, teaches that regularly. Who has to search for suffering? There is plenty of it in the normal experiences of life. The great lesson in suffering is we find out there is more to us than we knew.

> *"Character cannot be developed in ease and quiet. Only through experience of trial and suffering can the soul be strengthened, ambition inspired, and success achieved."* (Helen Keller)

If we walk through our fear of loss, if we embrace the darkness that sometimes surrounds us, we begin to detect the light that fills even the most remote corners of our fear.

> *"Who sees all beings in his own self, and his own self in all beings, loses all fear."* (Isa Upanishad, Hindu Scripture)

Our lives are layers of depth. As we penetrate one, we begin to see the next. Much like an onion, we peel away layer by layer until we reach the heart and the core. We are deeper than we ever imagine and the strength at our core that emanates outward is one sure place where we encounter the divine. We know ourselves and embrace our humanity when we learn to befriend our suffering.

> *"The most beautiful people we have known are those who have known defeat, known suffering, known struggle, known loss, and have found their way out of those depths."* (Elisabeth Kubler-Ross)

Suffering is clearly something we try to avoid. We fear the potential loss it might bring. But when we embrace our suffering and allow it to become our teacher, we grow in our ability to empathize and in our capacity to love.

> *"Empathy is really the opposite of spiritual meanness. It's the capacity to understand that every war is both won and lost. And that someone else's pain is as meaningful as your own."* (Barbara Kingsolver)

Each of us has a spiritual center that only suffering can begin to reveal.

The Catalyst Way

At a meeting one evening, two young Catalyst girls addressed a group from the surrounding community. They described the anxiety and burden they carried with them to the school each day. They knew, as Latino youth, their parents would be present to them in the morning but they never knew if they would be there when they returned in the afternoon. Arrest and deportation were a potential reality each and every day. Their suffering met love in the embrace of their teachers, who realized that this kind of anxiety-induced suffering really affects student performance even though state and federal educational bureaucracies and legislatively mandated testing rationales suggest it ought not matter. Real-life distraction of this proportion is stressful and interferes with the concentration needed to succeed. Provision for counseling, an understanding teacher, extra help, and building a supportive community—all help the distressed student walk into and through this suffering and begin to see their true strength that gives them the ability to bear it and to thrive.

"Out of suffering have emerged the strongest souls; the most massive characters are seared with scars." (Khalil Gibran)

3. Internal Struggle: Proverbs 16:32 says it: "The patient are better than warriors, and those who rule their temper, better than the conqueror of a city."

Our problems and our grief aren't most significantly those presented by the external world. Our issues are almost all internal, attitudinal, and emotional, about our frame of mind and how we look at things. How we deal with our issues involves personal choice. We carry our issues with us. I can sit in Chicago and nurse my problems and if I move to San Jose or New York City, I simply carry those problems with me. They may be presented in a different form, but ultimately they are me. The challenge is to build an internal sense of self-control. As adults, this is something we continue to master and it is something we must teach our young from the moment they are presented to us. Self-control, as Brooks says, builds an inner structure of depth.

Lasallian educators "school" our scholars in more than academics. The Lasallian school is a school for life and so developing those qualities and internal controls that lead to long-term success, long-term love relationships, long-term happiness are essential. Classroom management, codes of conduct, and disciplinary procedures are best when designed to lead students to critical thinking, analytical skills, and awareness that their behavior and conduct have significant impact beyond themselves.

The LaSallian Way

Brother Agathon, one of De La Salle's successors, described ten conditions required for discipline to be effective. Seven of them apply to the adult administering discipline and three to the student being corrected. The adult must make sure the intent is pure and not motivated by revenge or resentment; the administration must be charitable; the punishment must be just and may err on the side of leniency but never on the side of severity; it must be proper, that is, proportionate to the fault; moderation is key in disciplinary action, avoiding harshness; disciplinary action must be peaceable and devoid of impatience, rudeness, or agitation; and finally, it must be prudent, meaning the motivations of the child being punished must be understood by the one administering the punishment. The three conditions applicable to the child are that the child receive the punishment voluntarily, respectfully, and in silence.[6]

In this way, discipline is a teaching tool that attempts to help a student understand him or herself better. Discipline is one essential tool in helping a student wrestle with those internal dispositions that distract from becoming one's best self. At Catalyst, peace circles are often used to help students address these conditions as well as their own internal motivations and issues. This method also involves a student's peers in the process of correction and leads to more critical thinking and higher-level moral development.

The school built on the Lasallian tradition is inclusive in the development of its codes of conduct and disciplinary procedures. The Rules of Student Conduct provided by the public school district must reflect these conditions or the school creates its own such rules. Teachers participate in the development of procedures and policies governing student behavior. Parents are aware of how the school's educational team monitors and supervises students throughout the day. The foundational principle is that any policy or procedure keeps the school's primary goal in mind—the education of the whole person—and this means disciplinary rules, like other policies and procedures, are teaching tools through which the adults attempt to raise up the young to responsive and responsible adulthood.

"Self-control is one mark of a mature person; it applies to control of language, physical treatment of others, and the appetites of the body." (Joseph B. Wirthlin)

---

6. Brother Agathon, FSC, *Twelve Virtues of a Good Teacher, Postscript, Discipline and Correction*, Melun, Feb. 12, 1785, trans. and ed. by Brother Gerard Rummery, FSC. This English edition of the classic text by Brother Agathon, fifth Superior General of the Brothers of the Christian Schools, describes in detail the virtues of a good teacher in accordance with the listing by Saint John Baptist de La Salle in *The Conduct of the Christian Schools* (1706) and *Collection of Short Treatises* (1711). Originally printed some 100 years after the first Lasallian schools, "it affords a kind of benchmark by which to judge the fidelity of the Institute to the founding vision," according to Brother Rummery.

4. Obedience: This is the place where our internal gift encounters the world's need. It is why we are born. It is the calling, the vocation that is offered us and to which we are compelled to respond. Satisfaction and happiness are shallow if we refuse to be owned by our calling. Obedience to my calling is obedience to life. Brooks says this is not the same as the popular refrains, "follow your passion" or "listen to your own drum beat." Instead, the starting point is listening to what life asks of us. This calling is our passion and it is this vocational call that is the drum beat to which we move forward if we are to really find happiness.

We have a distorted notion about what obedience is. In too many corners obedience is about domination and submission—the power to control. Government, civil and ecclesial, and many other social and economic systems seem to be built on this twisted notion. More true to its meaning, and more fundamentally, obedience is about listening and responding. Most important is that we learn to listen to the way life calls us beyond our limited personal pleasures into the service of humankind and the world.

The challenge for educators is to discern, along with a student, what gifts he or she brings into the world and where that gift meets the world's need. Life isn't simply a matter of doing what I want. We are happiest and most fulfilled when we respond with our whole being to the needs of others. Obedience places us at the disposal of real need. Given this, how do we help our students understand themselves so they begin to get a real sense of their place in the world and find ways to fulfill their purpose in life?

The Catalyst Way

Catalyst Schools emphasize more than classroom success or standardized test scores.

- The homeroom teacher mentors a specific group of students.

- A course was developed that assists students to think about their futures and includes field trips, visits to universities, exploration of world issues, and an invitation to think about the person they want to be beyond high school.

- After-school programs involve students in a variety of activities. The Ravinia outdoor concert venue in Chicago initiated an orchestra with Catalyst elementary students (the largest all-African

American school orchestra in the country, according to Ravinia personnel). The Joffrey Ballet sent teachers to work with first-grade boys and girls and nineteen of those children were invited to join the Joffrey School.

- Both elementary and high school students meet their political representatives and talk about the needs of their community.

All of these things contribute to the generation of dreams that can carry a child into a sense of self and a future filled with hope and a sense of belonging.

"Everyone has his own specific vocation or mission in life; everyone must carry out a concrete assignment that demands fulfillment. Therein he cannot be replaced, nor can his life be repeated, thus, everyone's task is unique as his specific opportunity to implement it." (Viktor E. Frankl)

Catalyst attempts to inculcate not just academic success but a sense of purpose beyond academic attainment.

Students, parents, and staff from Catalyst Circle Rock who are members of the Ravinia Circle Rockets Symphony Orchestra visit the Ravinia venue north of Chicago.

5. Acceptance: Brooks rightly says that unconditional acceptance is what one hopes to find in family and unconditional support is also what a student should find in his or her school. Acceptance, like love and suffering, is a pure gift. There is little we can do to earn it. We have all met someone who just tries too hard to be liked. As a matter of fact, the harder we devote our lives to being accepted the more frustrated we can become. However, when we are blessed to receive acceptance, there is little to do but be grateful, appreciate it, and find ways to extend it.

Through acceptance, we discover that we are more than ourselves and are, in fact, connected to the whole of creation as we experience it and to those dimensions of the universe that are beyond our experiential knowledge. Acceptance is foundational. It teaches us forgiveness, gratitude, and delight, and leads to love.

Acceptance can bring us to a true humility because we know we have not merited it. It is simply a gift given gratuitously. This is why De La Salle worked so diligently to help his teachers understand the importance of their relationship with each student. The unconditional love of teacher for student demonstrates and models the way life can be and prepares the student to gift others in the same way. The gratuity De La Salle felt was so important might have had something to do with unconditional acceptance and inclusion. In the Lasallian school, no one is excluded. All are accepted.

The Catalyst Way

Every child is known by name and made to feel welcome, beginning with the handshake and "good morning" they receive when entering the building each day. It is not uncommon to see the dean of students with his or her arm around a child who is in trouble or feeling anxious. Differentiation is a hallmark of good teaching and Catalyst teachers are attuned to this as evidenced in the lesson plans they turn in each week for critique and support by their administrators. Each child receives special attention in the world of academics as they do in all other areas of school life. In the high school, parent conferences are completely student led, which gives students an opportunity to showcase their accomplishments to their proud parents. Homerooms are named after specific universities, creating a more intimate sense of community than all-school assemblies and events, as well as building an attitude of possibility and hope for success. Community is at the heart of acceptance and the heart of culture. It is important to do everything possible to invite a student to be a participating member of the community, to be him or herself, and to grow in confidence that this self is loveable.

Circle Rock founding principal Sala Sims congratulates an eighth-grade graduate.

"Unconditional love really exists in each of us. It is part of our deep inner being. It is not so much an active emotion as a state of being. It's not 'I love you' for this or that reason, not 'I love you if you love me.' It's love for no reason, love without an object." (Ram Dass)

When these five ways of interacting with life are modeled and taught, the school becomes an educational resource for the whole person and not just the intellect. The school prepares students exceptionally well academically but also attends to the spiritual journey inward toward an integrated self where the Spirit is encountered. When the conditions are set up for students to genuinely and honestly experience these five realities, they become paths to a deep sense of awe, gratitude, and trust that are the foundations of faith.

Love, Suffering, Internal Struggle, Obedience, Acceptance Leading to Awe, Gratitude, and *Trust* provide the fertile ground needed for faith to blossom, for real connection to be made, for us to believe that there is more to life than ourselves. These are the experiences that are essential in the formation of good people, of change agents who know the value of giving back to their communities. These are the experiences that allow us to say in eulogy, she was a wonderful human being who selflessly lived for others, who contributed to the welfare of the whole, who revealed the light in the darkness, who made each of us feel loved, who when we were with her we were at home.

These attitudes and dispositions toward life are the companion to academic excellence. They prepare children, adolescents, and young adults for the gift of faith. When educators are living their vocation, they are opening up a world of spiritual living for their students. Education of this magnitude requires healthy adults who have explored their own inner self and who know who they are. Education of this depth demands zealous teachers capable of authentic and gratuitous love for their students.

The experience of faith is the reconnecting to our essential nature that Rabbi Cooper speaks about. It is a journey and not a once-and-for-all given. It is not about doctrine or the acceptance of dogmatic statements so much as about pilgrimage and intentional discovery. Faith is about hearing, knowing, transcending, being, and it implies movement, action. The experience of reconnecting to our essential nature is a process of allowing the mysteries that life is and teaches to touch us. When we open ourselves to life's dynamics and surrender to its lure we are transformed. Faith is transformation. In some ways, the experience of faith is the experience of seduction. When we open ourselves to that which is beyond the material stuff we think is so important, we begin to discover the wonders "eye has not seen, and ear has not heard" (1 Corinthians 2:9). The experience of faith makes us a new creation.

Faith as Experience

When we talk about faith in schools, the controversy typically focuses around doctrine and whose belief system should be taught. This is, of course, why evangelizing or proselytizing is not permitted. Someone's first amendment right would be violated.

The LaSallian Way

Hiring for mission is critical in schools rooted in the Lasallian tradition. Seeking teachers who have the innate, even if not articulated, sense that they are teachers by vocation and not simply people who need a job is a priority for the school leadership team. A teacher in a Lasallian school is expected to have appropriate and healthy love for children and adolescents and to understand that he or she is more than a transmitter of information. In fact, one of the most important roles of the teacher imbued with Lasallian values is to mentor and guide students to healthy adulthood and to help them develop the skills needed to navigate these five core human experiences. When we hire men and women who are not only competent in their academic discipline but who grasp the importance of their presence in the lives of the young, the school thrives.

Hiring for mission is also why ongoing formation for mission is so critically important. Calling the educating community back to its common mission, continually teaching them about the roots and goals of the early Lasallian community, allowing them to explore such content as the principles of good discipline, the conduct of schools, the virtues of a good teacher, what it means to be a real person and not just a role, focuses the entire community's attention on why those who embrace the Lasallian Way are educators in the first place and what it means to be a teacher by vocation. Professional development beyond the latest teaching technique, newest set of standards, or the "how-to's," builds community around common values and has a great impact on the culture of the school.

The Catalyst Way

*A*t Catalyst, science classes can lead students to significant questions about their place in life as they explore the universe and realize that while we know a lot, we really don't know much. Literature asks students to embrace some of life's big questions about love, relationship, and dealing with the hardships life inevitably brings our way. Other courses explore the mathematic constructs that explain the structure of life. Catalyst hires teachers who understand the depth of their discipline and also that life is mystery, teachers who do not hide from the unknown, teachers who are not afraid of questions and who don't pretend to have all the answers. These teachers come to their work as full human beings, real persons, and not simply playing the role of teacher. They help students find comfort in the ambiguities and the uncertainties at the heart of living. Beyond delivering content, the primary role of teachers is to know their students personally and to walk with the young as they try to navigate their life circumstances.

Catalyst Maria students participate in a science lesson.

But what if the conversation took a different direction and instead of focusing on dogma and encouraging students to accept particular doctrinal articles of faith, we began to talk about how we walk with children into the questions about life with which all of us wrestle. When we speak at the level Rabbi Cooper and David Brooks are advocating the question of faith takes on completely different hues. We don't need answers. We need comfort with ambiguity, with doubt, with mystery, with things we don't understand. More important than answers to questions, young people need adult models that demonstrate it's possible to stand before the universe with open arms and who relax their defenses long enough to experience real transformation. Children need to know that long enough is a lifetime and not a day or a week. Transformation doesn't happen according to our academic expectations for the week. It's different for each person. It has its own time line we can only be open to and not control.

What Does This Mean?

Since the time of De La Salle in the late seventeenth and early eighteenth centuries, our scientific perspective has taught us new things. Our cosmology has evolved since De La Salle was alive. We realize more about the dynamics of the universe and the laws that govern it. We speak about faith and the experience of faith differently as well. De La Salle was born shortly after Galileo championed the Copernican revolution. Prior to Copernicus, people still thought Earth was the center of the universe. Just as our understandings of the world have changed, our perceptions about life and about God ought to be different as well.

Faith in light of what science has taught us about the universe becomes the very dynamic of transformation and of reconnecting with our essential nature. Transformation implies openness and vulnerability. It means we are receptive to what is new and to ways of perceiving that might make us uncomfortable. When we view life as a pilgrimage or journey we are willing to walk into the unknown. God told Moses to take off his shoes because the ground he was standing on was holy (Exodus 3:5). Unlike the tourist, the pilgrim understands that all ground is holy. It is the pilgrim's openness and vulnerability that allow him or her to experience meaning and depth. Giving up our attempts to control that which cannot be controlled is critical. Learning to shut up long enough to listen and opening our clenched hands long enough to receive is central.

A "Public" Experience of Faith

What are the dynamics of faith—rooted in the inward journey—that might be welcome in public education?

When we speak about things like love, suffering, inner control, obedience, and acceptance, we are entering a world of mystery, which is a world of awe, gratitude, and trust. Are these not the essentials of faith? Are they not the essentials of human relationship? Are they not the foundation stones for how we care for the world in which we live?

Marci, the wife of one Catalyst administrator, demonstrates an understanding of this when she speaks about Eucharistic Adoration. "We respect and adore the body of Christ when we respect and show deep appreciation for each of our students and their families. This is the adoration expected of us. God does not want sacrifice but wants service with the poor." When we understand that faith is about life and how we live it, it informs everything we do and how we treat every person we meet.

What other dynamics of faith might inform the public educator and the public charter school inspired by the Lasallian tradition?

Mystery

First, as educators who operate a school we are well aware that there is more to life than meets the eye. We are cognizant that not everything that matters is visible. There is a dimension to reality that always remains a mystery and that draws us beyond ourselves. The educational enterprise is anchored in that sense of mystery. Great literature abounds with references to it. Science exposes it. Math is the language of the universe. With it, we can understand the basic construction of our home in the cosmos.[7]

All that we know and all that we have learned as a human community points us in a direction and along a path whose destination is not yet experienced or attained. De La Salle would call the source and destination of our journey God. But whether we name that reality or believe in God or not doesn't change the fact that there is something in human experience that suggests there is more than what we physically touch, smell, see, hear, and taste.

Awe

Faith is rooted in awe. And when we view the universe, when we cross the painted desert, when we peer into the Grand Canyon, when we climb

---

7. For more from this perspective, see http://www.fromquarkstoquasars.com/why-does-mathematics-explain-the-universe/.

Mount Shasta, when we see a flower budding in the spring and what weeds grow from concrete in the summer, or when we fall in love or have any other profound human experience, how can we know anything but awe? Life is filled with wonder and amazement. It is bigger than us.

The Lasallian school encourages activities that put the entire community in touch with awe, with the magnitude of the symphony of which we are a part. The education provided offers a glimpse into worlds not yet experienced and a deeper understanding of those dimensions we do know. If we do not end our instruction with a question mark, we have not been educating. We rouse doubt, intrigue, and curiosity. We put students in touch with the mystery in life. We get them to stand back in wonder.

The Catalyst Way

When we witness the magnitude of life and how it manifests itself in nature, in relationships, and especially in our children, we are often brought to a sense of awe that is reverence. We experience deep wonder. We touch the mystery that is life.

A good teacher's sense of reverence is interior and sincere. It is also outward and a good example to children. The teacher exhibits the sentiments that fill his or her heart in the attentiveness given to each child's specific need and the patience exercised in engaging students in classroom activity and discipline. The teacher demonstrates reverence for students as persons, knowing their name, their family and social context, their motivations and their hopes for the future. Reverence means the work of teaching is personal. It is all about building relationship.

In her work as a Catalyst school secretary, Ms. Glover demonstrates respect daily. She says it this way: "Even though it gets really busy many times, the main thing is I have to smile because it can get overwhelming. Children need a band aide, a mother needs to deliver a message to her daughter, teachers want copies. Sometimes I am juggling multiple tasks but the most important thing is to remember how I want to be treated. I treat people this way. I smile because it gives people energy. When kids come to the office I talk with them. I ask them what they are doing. These students don't have a village to support them. We are their village."

Ms. O'Neil, a teacher, expresses her understanding of what showing respect for students means in this way: "We believe our children are capable regardless of their circumstances. I push and interact with my kids the same way I do with my own kids. I'm going to push for that excellence regardless of the system that is in place. Education is a tool—not only to get out but to give back. I tell my kids they are not 'less than' and that they need to step into their best selves."

Ms. Glover and Ms. O'Neil demonstrate the kind of reverence all employees are asked to embrace and to live at Catalyst Schools. Ms. Glover, no less than Ms. O'Neil, is an educator.

Mrs. Royal demonstrates reverence for her Catalyst Circle Rock kindergarten students by patiently helping them take the initial steps toward becoming readers.

Reverence

Reverence means to have feelings of deep respect or devotion. This sense of respect includes awe and even a sense of love.

Why is it important for reverence to be part of a school's culture? How are things different when this deep sense of respect, devotion, awe, and love are nurtured, encouraged, and articulated?

Reverence is foundational for living the Golden Rule of treating others as you want to be treated. When the members of the school community have reverence for one another and for their community, justice and peace reign, learning can happen, and success becomes standard.

Without reverence a school has no soul.

Gratitude

Awe can lead us to gratitude. If we experience the awe of our union with all of life and know that we are part of the great symphony of the universe, can we be anything but grateful? If we are allowed to doubt what we know and are encouraged to be curious about what is still unknown, aren't we in a place where gratitude becomes a common experience? In that kind of place, I can be who I am because nothing is finished or complete. Everything is in the process of becoming. And when the adults in my life know that each of us is an emerging creation, I am accepted and supported unconditionally. Questioning, dialogue, exploration, and discovery are not only expected but nurtured in a Lasallian school. Surprise becomes a daily experience. "Ah-ha!" moments are happening in every classroom every day. The school is filled with excitement that can barely be contained.

Administrators walk with teachers who walk with students into the unknown so everyone can learn something new. We get our scholars to stand back and to express gratitude for their very being and their participation in the magnificence of creation. We begin to see life as a great adventure into the infinitely knowable.

Activities outside of academics also promote a deeper understanding of life. Peace circles, for example, allow students to become more aware of their common humanity, similar dreams and desires. Dialoguing with classmates, students can engage emotionally, psychologically, and personally more regularly than in a classroom context. They begin to learn the great unity that underscores diversity and uniqueness. Celebrations of academic success, of co-curricular or extra-curricular achievements, also build student self-esteem and bring joy to families and communities. And when teachers are appropriately mentored and coached they begin to understand they are part of a community that sees the success of one as the success of all. All of this and more can rouse a sense of thankfulness in the hearts of teachers, students, and their families.

The Lasallian school must lead everyone associated with it to a sense of awe about the magnitude of life and how we are a part of it and then to deep gratitude for the gift received each and every day that is a new learning experience.

Trust

When we are filled with awe and gratitude we learn we can trust in the power that surrounds us and believe it will benefit and not harm us, even when life is painful. Our suffering is also a gift through which we learn who we are. Some call this stance trusting in Providence. It was a critical element in De La Salle's faith. He never made any significant change in his life without long periods of prayer and only after testing his intuition against the counsel of trusted advisors. In these ways, he believed he was in union with the movement of the Spirit of God and that this would inevitably lead him along the right path. He says,

> God who guides all things with wisdom and serenity and whose way it is not to force the inclinations of persons, willed to commit me entirely to the development of the schools. He did this in an imperceptible way and over a long period of time so that one commitment led to another in a way I did not foresee at the beginning.[8]

Trust in Providence was not religious magic for De La Salle. It was focusing attention on a concern, doing critical analysis, judging behaviors and their potential outcomes, and seeking the wisdom of trusted others—all in a spirit of openness, self-abandonment, and consideration of what could be the greatest good consistent with his faith. For him the power that surrounds us is God.

Trust as part of the experience of faith means finding comfort in knowing life will be as it is meant to be and that we will somehow be part of the thriving evolution of its totality. It means using our faculties to explore our situation, our options for action and its potential consequences, considering what is best for the common good, and testing our intuition by seeking the advice of those wiser than ourselves.

Trust means being open to new information, knowledge, and experience. There is always more than any one person or group knows. Our best minds have barely touched the depth of reality. Fifty years ago we thought we had the universe figured out—fully understood. Then along came quantum

---

8. Luke Salm, FSC, *This Work Is Yours: The Life of St. John Baptist de La Salle,* (Washington, DC: Christian Brothers Publications, 1996), 4.

The LaSallian Way

The Lasallian school is one in which everyone works diligently to establish a communion of trusting relationships that mirror the reality that life itself is trustworthy. We build the kinds of relationships with students that free them to trust in us, in themselves, and in the ultimate goodness of life itself. When a student experiences this kind of relationship, she is eager to learn.

Certain structural elements practically express the kind of relationships that are important in the school. A graduate support team that monitors the school's graduates and offers them assistance as they move through high school and into college or skill training says that our relationship is real and that our concern for the welfare and well-being of the student goes beyond day-to-day contact. A staff person dedicated to community outreach engages parents and the neighborhood in a way that says the school is here for you. Community outreach brings the assets of the school to other community organizations and in turn invites those organizations to be part of the life of the school. Teachers regularly call parents with good news, not just news concerning discipline issues. Teachers let parents or guardians know their child is cared for, known, observed, and has worth. An administrator welcomes each child to the school each morning. Every child is known by name. Each child has a champion who advocates for his or her success as a person. In these ways, the relationship builds, grows, and deepens. Trust is built. In De La Salle's thought, these are some of the tools through which the adults begin to nurture the sacred space in which the student knows he or she is loved and in turn gives permission to the adult to be teacher or administrator—to be the leader.

physics, tossing all we knew into the air. Science is confirming in our day what the ancients believed long before us.

Our inadequate knowledge does not control life. The core of reality is something we participate in and we are better when we trust it and allow it to reveal itself. Believing we are in control is an illusion and efforts built on control are ultimately going to leave us pondering how we could have been so wrong.

Some would have us believe we need all the answers, as if we were going to be a contestant on *Who Wants To Be A Millionaire?* But we are at our best when we are seekers. Trust requires us to assume a receptive posture. Transformation requires trust.

Must we use the word *God* to teach trust in Providence? Wasn't there a time when God had many names? Wasn't there a time when we were even cautioned against using any name for God? Who or what is "I am who I am" (Exodus 3:14)? Do we need to proselytize to answer this? Must we step beyond the law to work toward this? Is faith in fact faith only when the correct words are used—especially if those words are such trigger points that they inevitably end up creating controversies that miss the point entirely? Saint Francis said we should "preach the Gospel always and only use words when we have to." It is not the intent of the school to indoctrinate but to liberate. Our lives, and not our words are the message. Students who experience love begin to know what love is. Walking with someone through their suffering allows them to learn from it. Discipline that teaches internal control and mutual listening prepares for life. Acceptance breeds love and trust. When we accompany scholars through these experiences we also create experiences of awe, gratitude, and trust—we do not need to use any proscribed religious words. Students will enter the mystery of life and accept responsibility for their own lives. They will see the wisdom of treating others as they want to be treated. They will be open to all of reality.

Zeal

In addition to awe, gratitude, and trust, faith in the Lasallian school is closely related to zeal. In fact, De La Salle found these traits inseparable. There could be no sense of awe, gratitude, and trust without an increasingly energetic motivation to act as though those things mattered. If we are truly awe-inspired and grateful, and if we truly trust in the providence of the laws and power of the universe, we get on with life in a way that manifests the spirit that animates us. If, in fact, our lives teach more than our words, the zealous educator lives intensely for the sake of his or her students. Teachers are raising up the next generations and creating the kind of world desired for their own children.

Possessing these characteristics that typify faith is not only possible in a public school, but what kind of school would it be if it did not have these traits? Without love, suffering, self-control, obedience, and acceptance leading to awe, gratitude, trust, and zeal, there would be no dynamism, no excitement, no intrigue, no curiosity, no significant questioning. School would be a boring place where no real education for a full and rounded life was taking place. The school would not be a human community.

De La Salle, with the first community of teachers, understood that their identity was teacher. Teaching was not something they did but rather it was who they were. They did not go home and throw that identity in the closet. When a man or woman is teacher by vocation, in their core identity they are zealous for the welfare of their students and treat them as they would treat their own children. Parenthood does not end at bed time. The teacher does not stop being teacher at 4:00 p.m. when most students leave for home. The excellent teacher carries the needs of the students within, constantly thinking of ways to reach and engage and promote their authentic academic, emotional, psychological, and interpersonal success. Authentic teachers plan for, assess, monitor, mentor, and honestly and genuinely care for their children. Building a relationship of trust is not a two-hour-a-day job. For the excellent teacher, for the teacher who embraces the Lasallian tradition, the effort rises out of the teacher's identity. It is not a job. It is a life.

Mrs. Myers embodies the kind of zeal De La Salle thought was so important. The parent of a Catalyst graduate, she was hired to be on the school's Community Outreach team. She articulates her understanding of zeal this way: "After the principal greets each scholar every morning, I'm the second person they see. I see what they are coming in with—the emotion, the tiredness, the hunger. Our message to the children is that they have somebody else who loves them. In this school they will be taught and disciplined and cared for. I was talking with a teacher who was having a rough day today. I ended up giving him a piece of candy and told him I hoped it would lift his spirits a bit. We are here to lift up the positive. I'm that vessel that tries to ensure people will be OK. In our work you need love for people. I'm going to love you no matter what. That means I'll go the extra mile."

The Catch

There is a catch, of course. We need to participate as pilgrims on the journey ourselves. There is no way to walk with children into these experiences if we are not capable of the pilgrimage ourselves. And, when we can participate, our relationships with each other and with our students change. There is a different dynamic. Authority is rooted in servant leadership and is not top-down but is more pastoral, more like the conductor of an orchestra bringing harmony rather than dissonance and conflict to the community. Discipline is always about teaching and not punishment. Structures are totally transparent, from budgeting to the way academic clusters are formed to the rules posted on the walls. Our culture is built on the notion that the school is a community, a network of personal relationships built on articulated and owned values. Curriculum, while required by state mandates, is related to and grows out of the educational and personal needs of the students. And, while assessment is critically important, a child is never equated with a test score. The school is helping parents and a neighborhood community to raise up human persons.

All these things mirror mission and create a dynamic human culture anchored in values. The organization becomes more horizontal. The tables at which we sit become round and not oblong. There is no front or back. There are no sides. Every voice matters. We know and behave as though we are all in it together. Many may find this frightening, and so it's difficult to accomplish. Many would rather hide behind power, bureaucracy, and false authority. Building this kind of community is challenging. The journey of faith is not for the insecure so expect challenges and obstacles where fear tries to control openness.

Faith and Inclusivity

In the ideal world, the public school is dedicated to inclusivity. All are welcome to the banquet of public education. The table is set. Respect is the primary ingredient that generates the wonderful sharing that is possible when people genuinely care, exercise compassion and empathy, and make room for and respect the uniqueness of each person.

One clear example of this was observed by Mr. Shamim, director of IT services for Catalyst Schools. "I saw one of our scholars helping a disabled student," he said. "I thought it was a clear demonstration of our spirit—treat others as you want to be treated."

Religion, however, has been left out of the banquet festivities. Possibly this is because all too often religion has been reduced to fundamentalism, and people have abandoned common sense and the wisdom of experience for the false security of a dictated set of beliefs. Conversion tactics have sometimes been coercive, even brutal. People have been slaughtered and force, humiliation, and other forms of coercion have been used in the name of religion. We have seen the destructive nature of rigid and ideological belief that has given rise to more than praise and glory. Many people have been exterminated in the name of religion when mixed with politics.

It is for good reason that public schools cannot promote any specific religious point of view or faith perspective. Religious freedom, the rights of the family, the dignity of the human person demand that each of us is permitted the responsibility to seek out our own religious path and expression, even if it turns out that that is none at all.

Importance of the Human Spirit

However, even though we cannot participate in *religious speak,* there is an innate quality to human nature that propels us to wonder, to question the meaning of life, to seek more than we can touch, and to ask questions to which there are no quantifiable or measurable answers. When schools only promote access to information and quantifiable knowledge to the exclusion of fostering wisdom, seeking that which cannot be named, plumbing the depths of the human heart, and building relationships, we imperil the system and endanger the students. We risk teaching that such things are out of bounds, that it is okay to have questions about grammar, math, and science but not about the human spirit.

We know too clearly what happens when we give rise to highly competent managers, administrators, businessmen and businesswomen, financial gurus, and political leaders who have no sense of their true selves, no moral compass, no sense that they are in relationship to anything beyond their own egos and ideology, and no connection to their own spiritual sensitivity. Martin Scorsese's *Wolf of Wall Street* tells the story of a brilliant scam artist who preyed upon unsuspecting victims. Abuse of drugs and sex, manipulation of money, and various other crimes are not limited to the activities of Wall Street in the persona of a Jordon Belfort. He might even be a minor player in the international drama that has given us genocide, wars, spying and espionage, terrorism, and the cultural imperialism that subjugates one group by another.

In an educational system that fears the fundamentalist perspective and the way organized religion often has been more a problem than a source of inspiration, administrators and teachers have been driven into fear of anything but facts, quantifiable data, measurable results, and what we can touch. Schools have become test factories with standardized testing dominating the entire educational process and school culture. In spite of what is said, teachers spend significant time prepping students for these tests—and there are many to prep for! Jobs are at stake and school will be shuttered if the students' performance on tests is not up to expectation. "Data-driven" is not bad, but schools only deal with one kind of data.

Many students, parents, and teachers saw No Child Left Behind as a detriment to the public education environment because of its overemphasis on standardized testing. Hopefully, the new Every Student Succeeds Act (ESSA) will ensure that more than student test scores will be used by states as a way to evaluate teacher performance and student success. The White House Office of the Press Secretary summarized some of the provisions of the new bill:

- Holding all students to high academic standards that prepare them for success in college and careers.
- Ensuring accountability by guaranteeing that when students fall behind, states redirect resources into what works to help them and their schools improve, with a particular focus on the very lowest-performing schools, high schools with high dropout rates, and schools with achievement gaps.
- Empowering state and local decision-makers to develop their own strong systems for school improvement based upon evidence, rather than imposing cookie-cutter federal solutions like the No Child Left Behind Act did.
- Reducing the often onerous burden of testing on students and teachers, making sure that tests don't crowd out teaching and learning, and doing so without sacrificing clear, annual information parents and educators need to make sure our children are learning.
- Providing more children access to high-quality preschool.
- Establishing new resources for proven strategies that will spur reform and drive opportunity and better outcomes for America's students.[9]

It is important to correct the notion that if it cannot be touched and manipulated, we don't want to deal with it. If it cannot be seen and tested, we are told to act as if it does not exist or at least has no educational value. There is no place for silence beyond the volume zero imposed in the halls. There is no room for reflection about who I am and what I am here for. The question might be asked, "What does any of that have to do with math, science, technology, or English?" Indeed, we have been forced to act contrary to our own intuition that life is about these things and much more than these things. And many of us have behaved this way for so long that we even believe that that which is quantifiable is the only thing that matters.

Good teachers join self, subject, and students in the fabric of life because they teach from an integral and undivided self; they manifest in

9. The White House Office of the Press Secretary, December 2, 2015, https://www.white-house.gov/the-press-office/2015/12/03/fact-sheet-congress-acts-fix-no-child-left-behind.

their own lives, and evoke in their students, a "capacity for connectedness." They are able to weave a complex web of connections between themselves, their subjects, and their students, so that students can learn to weave a world for themselves. The methods used by these weavers vary widely: lectures, Socratic dialogues, laboratory experiments, collaborative problem-solving, creative chaos. The connections made by good teachers are held not in their methods but in their hearts, meaning heart in its ancient sense, the place where intellect and emotion and spirit and will converge in the human self.[10]

There is a core human reality "that 'heart and soul' language points to." Diverse traditions have named this core differently. "Hasidic Jews call it the spark of the divine in every being. Christians may call it spirit, though some (e.g., the Quakers) call it the inner teacher, and Thomas Merton (a Trappist monk) called it true self. Secular humanists call it identity and integrity. Depth psychologists call it the outcome of individuation."[11]

However we name it, too often this core human reality has become a casualty in the street fight that is now public education. Many teachers in both public and private religious schools are good teachers. For some, however, this may be true in spite of the system. School boards vs. teacher unions or charter schools vs traditional public schools are the kind of conflicts that define the battlefield we call public education. Students are trapped by many adults who have subjugated conscience, community, and empathy for the sake of winning the battle over schools. Bureaucrats rather than educators control education.

> "Successful teaching and good school cultures don't have a formula," argued legal reformer Philip K. Howard, . . . "but they have a necessary condition: teachers and principals must feel free to act on their best instincts. . . . This is why we must bulldoze school bureaucracy. . . . Bureaucracy fails, in part, because it honors leadership as a primary quality over expertise, commits to ideological solutions without identifying and clarifying problems first, and repeats the same reforms over and over while expecting different results: our standards/testing model is more than a century old."[12]

---

10. Parker Palmer, "The Heart of a Teacher: Identity and Integrity in Teaching," Center for Courage & Renewal, http://www.couragerenewal.org/parker/writings/heart-of-a-teacher/.

11. Ibid.

12. P.L. Thomas, "Politics and Education Don't Mix," *The Atlantic,* April 26, 2012, http://www.theatlantic.com/national/archive/2012/04/politics-and-education-dont-mix/256303/.

Families are victims of a system dedicated to information and winning, of ideology over Socratic investigation and compassionate collaborative truth seeking. Politics is now the playing field upon which educational praxis and values are being played out and it's ugly.

> One side of the political argument that has been waging for decades says: "Public education is the most expensive 'gift' that most Americans will ever receive. Government school systems are increasingly coercive and abusive both of parents and students. Government schools in hundreds of cities, towns, and counties have been effectively taken over by unions, and children are increasingly exploited, thwarted, and stymied for the benefit of organized labor."[13]

Another perspective is this:

> Although previous research has suggested that urban school systems are largely insulated from electoral politics, urban school system policymakers are highly sensitive to community and professional pressures. The consequence is that reform efforts are more heavily influenced by political pressures than by educational considerations. District policymakers constantly embrace politically attractive changes, producing prodigious amounts of reform at a pace inimical to effective implementation. As a result these reforms do not significantly alter the nature of schooling but they do manage to frustrate, confuse, and finally alienate faculty. In fact, a state of constant reform is the status quo in urban school systems.[14]

Paul Till and Ashley Jochim capture the mood and dynamic in their article "Political Perspectives on School Choice." "The issues at stake in a conflict often evolve as parties with different agendas align with one side or the other. That is the basis of the adage, 'Politics makes strange bedfellows.' Thus, the scope of the conflict enlarges in two ways: more parties are brought in and the range of issues at stake broadens."[15]

---

13. James Bovard, "Teachers Unions: Are the Schools Run for Them?" Foundation for Economic Education, July 1, 1996, http://fee.org/articles/teachers-unions-are-the-schools-run-for-them/

14. Frederick M. Hess, *Spinning Wheels: The Politics of Urban School Reform* (Brookings Institute Press, Washington DC, 1998), 7.

15. *Handbook of Research on School Choice,* Mark Berends, Matthew G. Springer, Dale Ballou, Herbert J. Walberg, eds. (New York: Routledge, 2009), 3.

The institutionalized system we know as public education seems as if it has lost its way and children are the first casualties. Fear of the consequences of fundamentalism and political battles have stripped the schools of spirit.

Consequences of Ignoring Spirit

Look at the consequences when spirit is ignored. We live in a nation consumed by consumption. While the number of homeless makes it impossible to walk the streets without being approached for donations, there are also people who have multiple homes and even "houses" for the stuff they can't fit into their homes. While food pantries are running low because the number of hungry families has radically increased, obesity and its consequences are our number-one health problem and the inspiration for a reality television program called *The Biggest Loser*. There is something wrong with this picture. If someone wants two or three homes, that's their business. But the balance is all wrong. Even among the people who now have more disposable income than they ever had before, the level of content and happiness has not significantly increased. Income and happiness correlate "up to a point, but not beyond it," according to studies. "A bigger paycheck ultimately leaves many people no happier."[16]

So what are all this consumerism and accumulation and achievement in this culture about?

> The idea of "I SHOP, therefore I AM" is a fantastic ego boost, so what's not to like? . . . An obsession with owning things is a meager attempt to fill a vacuum. Buying that new computer or fancy car might momentarily shrink the hole. Yet, you quickly adapt to the new upgrades and the hole grows, enslaving you to earn higher and higher paychecks with no way out.[17]

One might consider those who, when faced with self, are dissatisfied and go out to buy a new shirt or blouse in an attempted grab at happiness only to find that after a couple weeks they also need a new pair of shoes. Things don't ultimately satisfy. The human heart and the human spirit are not content only with things that can be touched.

---

16. Bruce Stokes, "Happiness Is Increasing in Many Countries—But Why?" Pew Research Center: Global Attitudes & Trends, http://www.pewglobal.org/2007/07/24/happiness-is-increasing-in-many-countries-but-why/.

17. Todd Sain Sr., "Consumerism and the Pursuit of Happiness," Our Breathing Planet. com, http://www.ourbreathingplanet.com/consumerism-and-the-pursuit-of-happiness/#sthash.RDCK2bLc.dpf.

Even other people leave us wanting. Our desire and passion are bigger than the things we try to fill them with. We are simply wired in a way we have not been taught to understand by contemporary public education or far too many families that are busy keeping up appearances or running feverishly to be at the front of the line. One might simply ask, for what?

> What the research shows about schools of all types and in all locations is that the best of the lot share two main characteristics: They have exceptional teachers and appropriate moral climates. (The latter, often a product of small schools with communities sharing common values, tends to attract the former, exceptional teachers wishing to teach in such an environment.) What is equally certain is that the school's internal moral climate runs counter to that of the external culture, at least the prevailing popular culture. . . . With all the spotlights on educational reform, we might just pause and shine a light on ourselves: In a democratic society, schools reflect the character of the culture.[18]

The culture we live in has placed high value on financial success—the right home in the right neighborhood, a fancy car, perpetual youth through hair transplants or plastic surgery, constant upward mobility. Madison Avenue and Wall Street values have been internalized. However, true satisfaction and happiness come from the intangibles that are not readily or easily quantifiable, measurable, or easily described. Try to measure love. Measure gratitude. Measure grief. Measure any of the human emotions that create the more significant "stuff" of our daily drama and you come up short. We can place electrodes in the brain and understand how the synapses work but that doesn't tell us the whole story about who we are—ultimately.

> "Concepts define," he said, "To define is to destroy. Concepts dissect Reality. And what you dissect you kill."
>
> "Are concepts then quite useless?"
>
> "No. Dissect a rose and you will have valuable information—and no knowledge whatsoever—of the rose. Become a scholar and you will have much information—but no knowledge whatsoever of Reality."[19]

So what is the role of spirituality in a public school or any school for that matter? In a faith-inspired school, the adults should be walking with chil-

---

18. Patrick Bassett, "Why Good Schools Are Countercultural," *Education Week*, February 2002.

19. Anthony DeMello, *One Minute Nonsense* (Chicago: Loyola University Press, U.S. and Canadian edition, 1992), 17.

dren as they both attempt to encounter the rose. The journey toward a real encounter with all of reality is what education should be about. It's not a walk through our comfort zones and no more. If it is true to its tradition, a Lasallian school is countercultural and strives to help students understand the value of more than what the culture deems success.

Core Value: Gospel Values

De La Salle believed in the Good News of salvation as presented in the Christian Gospel. When he said the mission of the Christian School is the salvation of the young, he was speaking about introducing them to the values made explicit in the life of Jesus and bringing them into an intimate relationship with Jesus' person. De La Salle's meditations and interventions with his teachers are filled with scriptural images and references that illustrate these values and demonstrate what good behavior looks like.

In the context of public education, where it is not permitted to evangelize, these same Gospel values can still be valid. Because these values are articulated in Christian Scripture, does the source make the content invalid? Or can we speak about and present these substantive principles of life in ways that uphold their truth without evangelizing to any religious path? Might these values be some of those that a society can hold in common and that can be part of the formation of conscience so needed by the young who are entrusted to us by their families?

Proclaiming the Values of the Gospel

The following list of "Gospel Values" comes from A Sense of the Sacred, a web site that speaks to values education.[20] The list has been edited to remove references to "God" in order to demonstrate that such values can be taught in a secular as well as a religious setting. Others might choose to add additional values or to name these in different ways. But when the substance is examined, it seems they would be values we would want to hold in common for the strength of society and community. It would also be difficult to say they should not be taught to children or that children would not benefit from integrating them in their own worldview and personality.

Gospel values begin and end with the love that is recommended to us over and over again in the Christian Scriptures. In John's Gospel, Jesus says,

---

20. "Gospel values," A Sense of the Sacred, https://sites.google.com/a/syd.catholic.edu. au/a-sense-of-the-sacred/gospel-values.

"Whoever does not know love does not know God, because God is love" (1 John 4:8, New International Version).

If faith is really an experience and not a set of doctrinal statements, the same can definitely be said of love. It seems this may be what John is saying. In order to know who God is, it is essential to know and experience love. Unfortunately, our culture offers us mostly sentimental and sappy versions of what love is. Only the romantic versions of love are presented while the behaviors associated with the Gospel values named here are not.

Gospel Values	
Awe and Wonder	An ability to marvel at the complexity of the created world.
Celebration	Appreciating the human need to commemorate important events and life stages by various rituals.
Common Good	Total human well-being that takes into account the needs of the whole community. Individual rights must always be assessed in light of the Common Good.
Community	A sense of belonging among a group of people with a shared vision committed to loving service.
Conservation	Maintaining and cherishing what is good in the environment with a view to ecological/environmental sustainability.
Courage	Choices, commitments, and actions made in accord with what one believes to be true and right; a willingness to persevere in the face of suffering and opposition.
Cultural Critique	Informed awareness of the injustices and inequities in society and a willingness to work to change these.
Dignity of Each Person	Life is sacred. The basic source of human dignity lies in humanity's call to communion. Respect for life, and above all the dignity of the human person, is the ultimate guiding norm of any sound economic, industrial or scientific progress.
Family	However it is expressed or understood, the family is cherished and fostered as the primary unit of belonging in society. It assumes personal values of identity, love, commitment, and self-sacrifice.
Global Solidarity and the Earth Community	All creatures and all of creation are intrinsically valuable and linked.
Hope	A spirit of optimism and joy; an enduring and sustaining trust in the fundamental goodness of life.

Hospitality	An attitude of openness, understanding, and welcome to others.
Human Rights	All people have the universal human right to live with dignity and freedom from oppression.
Justice	The right ordering of relationships and right exercise of power in a way that is life-giving for all people.
Love	The gift of sincere care, concern, empathy, and compassion extended to others; love is patient, kind, humble, forgiving, and trusting.
Multicultural Understanding	Positive interaction with other cultures for mutual understanding and enrichment; an openness to and dialogue with those of different cultural backgrounds.
Peace	Peace is the fruit of justice and depends upon right order among humans and among nations; seeking peaceful, life-enhancing solutions to conflict; peace is more than simply the absence of war or conflict.
Reconciliation	Reaching out in a spirit of dialogue, forgiveness, and mutual respect; closely linked to love and justice.
Sacredness of Life	Seeing life as a gift to be respected.
Service	Loving care for the needs of others.
Stewardship of Creation	People respect and share the resources of the earth since we are all part of the community of creation. By our work we are cocreators in the continuing development of the earth.
Structural Change	Addressing root causes of injustice and changing unjust systems and structures; the transformation process that seeks a society that is life-enhancing for every person.
Self-Respect	• Proper esteem or regard for the dignity of one's character and person; • Due respect for oneself, one's character, and one's conduct; • The deep conviction of one's own inner worth; • The quality of being worthy of esteem or respect: "it was beneath his/her dignity to cheat"; "showed his/her true dignity when under pressure," etc. • A capacity to love others assumes self-esteem, that is, a felt sense of one's inherent confidence, dignity, and freedom. This is to value one's individuality and uniqueness.

As listed, each of these values is expressed as action: marvel; appreciate; assess; share vision; commit to service; maintain and cherish the environment; persevere in the face of suffering; work to change inequity; respect life and the human person; cherish our most important relationships; trust; understand and welcome others; extend compassion and empathy to others; dialogue with those different from us; seek peaceful solutions to conflicts; forgive; care for others' needs; change unjust structures; maintain respect for self.

Love is not a romantic feeling as much as it is a set of convictions about life and the person's place in it that are expressed in behavior. Love is active not passive. It seeks the best for the common good. When students grow in this kind of love, learning the value of these behaviors day by day, they become change agents in their communities.

De La Salle never thought of love sentimentally. When he encouraged his teachers to love the children he was encouraging these behaviors that rose from his reading of the Gospel. Once again, the purpose of the schools was the salvation of the young. When children are educated and embrace these kinds of values, they grow in wholeness and become productive, contributing citizens who are committed to more than their own welfare. They know that they are participants in a society and that the welfare of all is their concern.

These values can be proclaimed and taught without proselytizing. They are central to what it means to be human and social. If they are not being promoted, we are cheating children and sacrificing the welfare of our society. In their place is found selfishness and greed, hate and conflict, anxiety and alienation.

Core Value: Academic Excellence

Simply because a school, in order to achieve real quality, is focused on the intangibles and creates the experience of faith as embodied in awe, gratitude, and trust, does not mean there is no focus on solid academics accompanied by high expectations. If the salvation of youth means faith and practical skill, one without the other damages youth. The experience of faith, the journey into mystery, is the intimate companion of academic excellence.

In today's climate, excellence is often reduced to how well students score on a state or standardized test. While assessment is critically important it is not the final goal. De La Salle and the early teachers assessed student progress daily and also conducted more formal monthly assessments to determine overall progress and movement. But the early teaching community never viewed these assessments as an ultimate measure of success. Rather, success was understood in the context of mission. These Lasallians took the long view and never forgot the actual purpose of their work with children. Teaching was a generative vocation. These men were helping to lift up a new generation. They were providing life opportunity. They were changing the world. As a result, they viewed academic excellence in terms of the whole picture and not just curriculum or how students performed on a summative assessment. Academic excellence, a quality school, meant the entire reality, with the mission always at the core.

Quality Education

Stated very simply, "quality education" in the Lasallian schools means we develop and maintain diverse programs meeting recognized standards of excellence. The education offered is comprehensive and accessible as well as practical.

As Ms. Morgan, the community outreach director, reflected, "We put things in place that challenge the whole child. We want them to have the kind of educational experience we want for our own kids."

Philosophically, the Lasallian school takes each student seriously as the primary subject and agent of his or her own education. Each student is seen as unique and special—a gift to the world that is gradually being revealed and appreciated. The revealing takes place in community. The Lasallian school results from a community that has committed itself to function collaboratively and together. There are no "Lone Rangers." Responsibility is shared and the school is run by the entire educational community. Regular professional development programs built on expressed teacher needs, cluster meetings, consultations among principals, directors of instruction, coaches, and mentors—all give teachers an opportunity to voice their insights and desires, and to help the school build a common vision and commonly implemented policies and practices. At its core, the school is not owned by a Board, or a CEO, or a principal. The community—teachers, parents, administrators, students—experiences belonging and shared ownership for what happens on a day-to-day basis. It is in the community (those people who engage the children daily and adapt to the emerging and changing dynamics of daily life) where ownership is built. The school that offers quality education and academic excellence is not static but living and growing and deepening. It functions through the mutual commitment freely given by the adult educators who believe they are there to serve the families and the students who choose to attend.[21]

---

21. Paraphrased and adapted from Jose Maria Valladolid, FSC, "Distinguishing Characteristics of Lasallian Education," a position paper delivered at the 4th Congress of Lasallian Education in Bogota, Colombia, January 1991. Lasalliana 24-16-C-111.

Each scholar is a person, an individual with unique abilities, gifts, attributes, and needs. Children are not numbers or test scores. The young are not viewed as simply part of a group. Each student is known by name and has positive and healthy relationships with caring and interested adults who deliberately and intentionally learn about the context in which each child lives and grows, the learning style that suits her best, the academic capacity and needs she brings to the school and then develops while there.

Ms. Granger knows what this looks like. "Academically, socially, we have to network throughout the school. With special education specialists. With our after-school Renaissance partners like the Ravinia orchestra teachers, the director of the Chicago Children's Choir. We look for equal opportunity for all students. I work hard to make sure when I look at my students, I see them as individuals. I know each one's needs. This takes time and means building relationships with them. I learn to respond in a way, individually, that works for each student. My director of instruction helps me in reaching each student. Working together with my colleagues helps get to this goal as well."

The dean understands this as well. "We take a holistic approach, giving children and families an opportunity to educate the whole person. I do this in my role by building relationships with families. We have small, intimate sessions with them and explore their insights and also why we do the things we do at school. We learn a lot about the children by doing this."

A young musician with Catalyst Circle Rock's Ravinia Circle Rockets symphony gets ready for rehearsal.

The Catalyst Way

*A*t Catalyst Schools, designated staff function full time as community liaisons and attend community gatherings, join community organizations, take parents to their political representatives' office to voice their concerns, and work with local networks of schools to meet with the state legislature on behalf of education funding. These staff persons also connect with enrichment programs and bring them into the school as part of after-school programming for the enrichment of the students. Police departments conduct meetings for the community in the assembly room. The school joins forces with local community organizing committees. Teachers are on the streets before and after school and know what is happening. Parents who choose to send their children to the school are interviewed, meet teachers and administrators, tour the building, and visit classrooms. They go through an intense orientation. They are frequently in the building as volunteers. Parent/child breakfasts, family science, math, and reading nights are all ways to get to know families and the children in a different context. In these ways, the educational team becomes part of the community and knows the issues and the context out of which the children come to them.

Beyond Course Content

Academic excellence relates to much more than course content. It requires the community that is mutually committed to running the school to know the neighborhood and the social structure in which the children are being formed beyond the boundaries of the school. It requires the committed community to know something of the family life that promotes or inhibits the students' formation and learning. All of this is necessary because we cannot teach someone we don't know. We can throw information at them but that is not teaching. We cannot build trust with someone we do not care to know. In the Lasallian school, teaching is a relationship in which all are learners and all are teachers. When the teacher knows the student, she also learns how best to reach that child and to engage him in ways that open him up to those experiences of awe, gratitude, and trust while helping him embrace and understand the content of a particular class.

While much responsibility rests on the shoulders of the teacher, the students are not excused from personal responsibility for their progress. No matter what the scholar's age, he is expected to take up the duties learning imposes—hard work, application to the task at hand, active participation. From preschool and kindergarten through the primary grades and into middle school and then on to high school, students are nurtured and moved into an understanding that they can tackle difficult tasks and accomplish more than they thought they could. They are taught emotional balance and to maintain a positive spirit about themselves and the progress they are capable of making. Students are encouraged to take initiative, to be themselves, to ask difficult questions, to be open to discovery. Their curiosity is viewed in a positive light and not suppressed.

Academic excellence on the part of the student is no more a lone-ranger experience than is teaching for the educator. Students in a Lasallian school are also part of a community and are formed in the spirit of the Golden Rule. They experience themselves as a necessary part of a community of learners, and because they are connected, they also learn the value of treating one another as brothers and sisters. When the young become, in this way, good citizens of their school, they are also learning what it means to be good citizens in their neighborhood and city. They will become change agents who make a difference.

One of the Catalyst principals, Ms. Dunn, is clear about this. "I always think of our name *Catalyst,* an agent of change. We are here to form change agents. It is done through the work of our staff and what we try to instill in our students. They have the capacity to do anything they want in life and to become the hope of society. They have the power to impact what is going on around them. Personally, I am very mindful and deliberate with the people I allow to be with our children. I will not allow the children to be dissuaded from knowing they can achieve. I build stability in our team. I put a variety of programs in place for our children because you cannot be what you cannot see."

The Catalyst Way

Teaching personal responsibility to children is a daily challenge. The lesson begins with attendance, which is closely monitored. Being present is 90 percent of the battle for some of the students. Parents whose children are late receive a call so they understand what is going on. Regular homework is assigned and reviewed in class. Accelerated reading and math offer students some gradual independence in what they choose to read and the progress they make week to week. Learning centers encourage group activity and are one of the tools teachers use in differentiating instruction. Each child is met with high expectations for performance and is held accountable through the assignment of grades, regular reports to parents, and student-led conferences.

Restorative justice is a central feature of the disciplinary process and through it students are able to see each other as real human beings with needs, dreams, hopes, anxieties, problems, as well as personal and family struggles. The process of peace circles often turns enemies into friends, levels the emotional playing field, and enhances the health of the community.

Restorative justice and the peace circles are not the only tools that help students see themselves in empathetic relationship with one another. There are many ordinary ways community and relationships are built. The dynamics of diversified learning groups, discussion groups, homeroom teams, athletic teams, after-school groups (orchestra, drumming, choir, cooking, and more), service projects like assisting in a food pantry, planting a garden or repairing bicycles—

all bring students together with the adults in academic and nonacademic settings that provide opportunities for people to meet, to know one another, and to learn that there is support, help, and life in this specific school community. No one need be a lone ranger, isolated or lost.

A student watches and listens intently during a drumming lesson at Circle Rock 753. At Catalyst Schools, such activities bring students together with adults in academic and nonacademic settings.

Ambassadors for Mission

The teacher is an ambassador of the school's mission, which is the salvation of youth. This means each teacher must be fully prepared in his or her content area, excellent at helping students be vested in the educational process, and able and ready to serve as ministers who understand that scholars are not only engaging content but the fullness of life. The language arts or literature teacher helps expose children to the variety of ways authors see life.

The art or music teacher helps students tap into the creativity that gives birth to new realities. The science teacher ushers students into a world of wonder and magnificence.

Academic excellence and quality education are about discovery and the exploration of questions that often have no immediate answer. Quality education embraces ambiguity and helps the young find comfort in the great "in-betweenness" of life. We know some things but most things we don't know, so we keep exploring, keep learning, and stay excited. Quality education gives rise to lifelong learners who aren't finished on the last day of the last year of their academic career.

Education Is Personal

The adult educator is one who embraces each of his or her students as a big brother or sister. The good we want for students is the same good we want for our own family. The true educator is one who knows deep in his or her heart that he or she is a teacher by identity. It is a vocation, not a job. This kind of teacher never finishes the task because the effort is about flesh and blood and spirit—real persons. Students occupy the teacher's thoughts and reside in the teacher's heart from morning till night.

Saint John Baptist de La Salle sought this kind of teacher to be "brother" to the poor students who came to his schools. He often encouraged his brother teachers to make their students the core of their lives, the center of their prayer and contemplation. They were never a distraction from more important things because they were the most important.

De La Salle told his teachers that their own salvation was closely connected to the students themselves and possibly to those who were hardest to reach. Someone who is just doing a job typically does not understand this. The educator by vocation implicitly and explicitly knows that the purpose of life is being generative and raising the next generation. Teaching is all about giving life. The excellent teacher is a teacher inside and out and puts his or her self at the disposal of others and offers them freely what he or she has learned about life, knowledge, personal qualities, faith experience—the entire journey. The teacher is a person and the excellent teacher brings his or her full person into the classroom and enters into relationship with other real persons. The one who is teacher by vocation, the excellent teacher, does not play a role. De La Salle knew that it was the strong relationship between a caring teacher and a student that was the key to learning. That doesn't develop when a teacher plays at being a teacher, which is what happens when teaching is simply a job.

The Conduct (Management of the School)

Saint John Baptist de La Salle and the first brothers who ran the schools did so for thirty-five years before they began writing about their best practices. When they finally set pen to paper, they created a book called *The Conduct of the Christian Schools*. *The Conduct,* as it came to be called, outlined every dimension of the school and gave voice to what worked. *The Conduct* was the result of the lengthy collaboration between De La Salle and the classroom experience of his teachers. It is not based solely on theory. It was written, as was most all of De La Salle's work, based on lived experience. It outlines how the schools were managed with greatest effect.

The Conduct emphasizes a practical approach to education and this was how De La Salle formed his teachers. The school as community is seen in the fact that "De La Salle met frequently with the Brothers in an atmosphere of open discussion and participative decision making to improve upon the running of the schools."[22]

As has been noted, this practice continues at Catalyst. Weekly professional development, regular grade level cluster or departmental meetings, consulations with teachers, coaches, and mentors—all contribute to an atmosphere that promotes participative decision making.

This sense of community and embracing the evolution of the teachers' experience in running schools meant *The Conduct* never had a final form but was always in the process of revision so that ongoing experience could always be influential. Education was not static but dynamic and as society changed and circumstances developed so did the understanding of best practices. Moreover, this dynamism also indicated that De La Salle and the early leaders of his teaching community trusted the teachers. What teachers thought mattered because they were the frontline implementers. If anyone was to know what worked it would be the teachers.

An excellent school involves its teachers in evaluation and assessment of its internal structures and processes and relies on teachers' insights for improving. The Lasallian school is not a hierarchical system that hands everything from the top down. Rather, decision making and deliberation are inclusive. At Catalyst, teachers are frequently asked what they think through a variety of means such as at faculty meetings, in individual coaching meetings, and through Survey Monkey. Results of such input are shared with faculty and staff.

---

22. Edward Everett, FSC, "The Educational Background to John Baptist De La Salle's *Conduct of the Christian Schools,*" 1985, http://www.lasallian.org.au/public/resources/fetch.cfm?fid=-4D73AE0C-5004-2673-A7D79A67602A5D39. The full *Conduct of the Christian Schools* can be found at https://lasallian.info/wp-content/uploads/2012/12/Conduct-2007-reprint.pdf.

The LaSallian Way

Teacher Training: When De La Salle thought of a quality school, he considered multiple factors. The first of these was always about the person he placed before the children as their teacher. Lasallian historian Edward Everett, FSC, described training for the new teachers under De La Salle.[23] According to Everett, *The Conduct* was used as a training tool. De La Salle led the new, untried teacher through the school day. He taught them about classroom management—establishing the psychological, social-emotional, and moral atmosphere that was acceptable in the classroom. He taught them about managing space, time, and motion in the classroom. He worked with the new teachers to demonstrate appropriate student placement, good learning activities, and where the teacher should place himself in relation to the students. He taught scaffolding of content and differentiated educational approaches that suited each student's requirements. He taught appropriate learning centers and grouping of students with like abilities and needs. Teachers learned to engage students who had mastered content with those who were struggling. Ultimately what the new teacher was learning was the importance of the care that must be given to the assignment of each student to the right place, level, and appropriate lesson. These were all the conditions that had to be met before teaching and learning could happen. Without appropriate attention to these kinds of details there would be no learning for students and only frustration for the teacher. The necessary relationship would not be built between teacher and student.

Similarly today, when new teachers, or even teachers experienced in a different system, begin work at a Catalyst School, they

---

23. Everett, ibid.

are often surprised by the frequency of visitors to their classroom and meetings with members of the Catalyst leadership team, comprised of mentors, coaches, and directors of instruction. Teachers are encouraged in ways to engage and group their students, and assisted with classroom management, differentiation procedures, and strategies for relating to parents and guardians. There is a checklist about creating and maintaining a clean classroom, and what to put on the walls. The leadership team is dedicated to teacher success, which ultimately means student success.

School Community: De La Salle encountered challenges as he strove to create the kind of community he believed essential to academic excellence. We might recognize one or more of these roadblocks today: teacher inefficiency, neglect, and cruelty; and student disorder and absenteeism. De La Salle studied these obstacles carefully and, along with his teachers, devised strategies to mitigate their influence: vigilance, teachers well prepared for classroom instruction, prayer, and practical community-building strategies such as setting a good example for the students and their parents.

Vigilance, for example, is first of all an attention to detail. The vigilant teacher exercises foresight and invests more in prevention than in recovery. This involves knowing the students well enough to understand what motivates them and what kind of correction they respond to best; planning and investing time in creating lessons that engage, and being attuned to potential problems that could arise during the lesson. Vigilance is really about good service to students. The excellent school, because teachers were vigilant, had an atmosphere of calm and a sense of mutual engagement. Anxiety levels are reduced for teachers and students alike in such a school. Classrooms in De La Salle's day were crowded as they are today, and vigilance and calm were important for maintaining a productive system and avoiding chaos.[24]

The longest reflection in the second part of the Conduct concerns discipline, always critical when dealing with children. The school is a social structure and without discipline it can become anarchy. De La Salle was no fool. Talk about faith and good intentions always occurred in the context of what was real. And what was real was that De La Salle's students came to him from the streets, where they were living unsupervised lives and left to their own devices. Some were thieves with no moral compass. Part of nurturing the student meant the teacher had to have a father's firmness along with the gentleness of a mother.

Though corporal punishment was commonly accepted in seventeenth-century France, De La Salle frowned upon it. He advised his teachers that it had to be a last resort, used sparingly and infrequently, with great moderation, and in controlled circumstances. Eventually it was simply banned. Throughout his treatise on discipline, De La Salle makes it clear that there are generally two parties involved in every disciplinary situation and one of them is the teacher. Teachers are human. The beginning of every disciplinary event is that the teacher examines his or her own behavior and role in what might have given rise to a situation needing correction. De La Salle contended that only a pleasant and genuinely concerned teacher who is also competent keeps students from dropping out of school. For De La Salle, the teacher is the absolute key to an excellent school. Nothing else matters as much.

Teacher Support System: As a result, a strong teacher support system was seen as vital. For De La Salle this was the primary role of the head of the school, the administrator, or principal. This person

---

24. Everett, ibid.

should be a master teacher with sufficient experience with all the difficulties teachers encounter to be of use to them as they hone their skills and master their craft. Mentoring, coaching, classroom visits, teacher interviews, ongoing evaluation and assessment are not done to "catch" a teacher doing something educationally inappropriate but rather with the view of being helpful and assisting especially inexperienced teachers to discover their capacity for greatness. What the teacher does for students, the administrator does for teachers.

Academic Content: Regarding subject matter, De La Salle believed content should be practical. Remember that the salvation of youth meant making certain the young poor had the requisite skills necessary to get employment, to raise a family, and to get off and stay off the streets.

For example, teaching students to navigate a ship by use of the stars at night was absolutely practical in De La Salle's day. Calais was a port city in northern France and navigation was an important industry. For students at the school De La Salle established there, learning these skills meant a future. For other students, bookkeeping and even penmanship might spell the difference between a life of poverty or being a contributing and satisfied member of society.

Curriculum for the Twenty-First Century

Curriculum development evolves as need evolves. What was practical in one day may not be in another. Today, STEM (Science, Technology, Engineering, and Math) might be a critical course of study if students are going to be prepared for employment in the twenty-first century. As a result, Catalyst has hired teachers specifically dedicated to STEM education. Computer programs, 3D printers, and well-equipped science labs offer high-quality exposure to these important fields. Technology has become critical in life and so must be embraced in education as well. Every classroom has a

SMART Board™. Each student has an iPad. Kindergarten students learn to manipulate technology. Many students' homes lack these resources, so it is important to provide them. A neighboring hospital as well as other partners in education expose students to a variety of experiences and career choices that help the school educate the whole child. The first Lasallian teachers could not have conceived of such things. Today they are commonplace.

© Mike Fehrenbach, FSC

Catalyst-Maria high school students do research during a classroom activity.

The critical take-away, it seems, is the view that salvation includes an education that prepares students to enter life in practical ways. Lasallian schools encourage skill building that prepares students for jobs that pay a living wage. A Lasallian education teaches critical thinking so that students can engage in serious inquiry and reflection in school and beyond. The Lasallian school teaches higher level thinking. It is important for students to learn the building blocks for analysis, evaluation, and synthesis. We are not training parrots but human beings who will be fully engaged citizens, political leaders, managers of industry, scientists, lab technicians, medical professionals, teachers, artists, and a myriad of other vocations that will give direction to the growth and development of society. We need competence and the ability to think beyond the currently experienced boundaries of our knowledge.

An academically excellent school does these things. It is a reflective and calm community that discerns, over time, the best practices most suited to its situation and its students. The Lasallian school is diverse and accessible. It takes students seriously as real persons. The school is in a relationship with the neighborhood in which it resides. It ensures that students little by little become responsible for their own learning, and become self-disciplined and self-directed as well. It expects teachers to take ownership for the community that engages students and walks with them into the wondrous ambiguities and intangible dimensions of life while preparing them for creative and productive employment. It is a horizontal system where all voices matter, and never only a disinterested hierarchy that lays burdens upon anyone. Responsibility and decision making are shared. The school is attuned to ongoing developments and evolves its curriculum to meet projected needs.

The Lasallian school, in the final analysis, is always about the salvation of youth; that means, in part, excellent preparation for a productive and satisfying life.

Core Value: Inclusive Community and Respect

Teaching can be an isolated and isolating experience. Planning for the week can happen at home and alone. A teacher can be, in some ways, the king or queen of the land. She rules the landscape of the classroom. The call for volume 0 goes out and the expectation is quiet will result; a noncompliant child is disciplined. Sometimes the teacher does not even see his colleagues during the day, the demands of teaching devouring time, as well as the teacher's physical and emotional energy. A Lone Ranger attitude can creep in and eventually a teacher can begin to feel and believe that he is in it alone and that success or failure is solely the individual's responsibility. But the school is a network of relationships and not an individual's isolated experience. The faith-based or faith-inspired school, the quality school, is built upon a deep sense of community.

Inclusive Community and Respect for All Persons

When John Baptist de La Salle first began to address the educational needs of the poor boys of Rheims, teaching was indeed an individual and isolating work. Seventeenth-century educational models put one instructor with one student and together they pounded out the lessons. A room could be filled with children but a Writing Master would still work with them one at a time. Chaos might be the atmosphere, confusion the ambiance, dysfunction the rule.

Teachers were not necessarily much more educated than the children they were instructing. The job of teaching was viewed as the bottom rung of any career ladder and occupied by those who could do nothing else. Teachers were ill respected and ill paid. In the caste system of seventeenth-century France, teachers were among those at the bottom of the heap. They were neither nobility nor clergy. They were nothing.

As De La Salle gradually entered the world of education, he began to see the need for a new praxis. Children were unsupervised and raising themselves on the street. There was no benefit to an educational system that simply allowed the same lack of discipline. He saw the difficulties of teachers, and the deficits created in the way teachers viewed themselves and how they were viewed by society. The whole system was bad and of no real benefit to anyone, including the teacher, who was barely paid enough to hold body and soul together.

Elevation of the Teacher

De La Salle, who was from the clergy and wealth, came to understand the priority need to change how teachers were perceived, both by society and by themselves. He began training them. De La Salle himself commented that the first men gathered to become teachers were of lower estate than his own valet. They had little education, and no sense of gentility, manners, or etiquette. They were rough and uncouth. De La Salle's task was to elevate them, to bring them to some sense of their own worth and dignity.

His theological training and his faith told him that these men were unique in the eyes of the God who created them. They had inherent value simply because they were alive, and their lives had purpose. He wanted to help them see that value and that purpose, believing that once they did, their talents and gifts would be freed and available for the benefit of others. Moreover, De La Salle believed the purpose of education was the salvation of youth. How could teachers who were uneducated and had no sense of their own value help the young who were poor, unsupervised, unscrupulous, and also at the bottom of the social structure? Unless the teachers had faith, they could not lead the children to faith. Unless the teachers had a moral compass, they could not begin to develop that in their children. Unless teachers had competence and were educated, they had nothing to teach that would have value to the poor boys that came to them for instruction.

And so, De La Salle set upon the first and most important task in his educational mission: He had to train and elevate teachers to a level of competence and self-respect that would give them requisite skills and a sense of purpose. The result would be that they could accomplish a most valuable mission—saving children. De La Salle believed every child deserved an excellent teacher who saw value in that child, who saw the child's potential, who knew how to touch that child's mind and heart.

The initial teaching corps gathered by De La Salle were housed together both for economic reasons and the convenience of location near the school in which they were teaching. Because teaching was such taxing work, and because De La Salle had not resigned from his other jobs as priest and canon of the Cathedral (a paid ecclesial position), there was little time to do the formation work that seemed so necessary. So he took a bold step. He began inviting these men into his family home for meals. This gave him more time to work with them and to talk with them about their mission and their own behaviors in relationship to their work and the children. Once he did this, his relationship to the teachers and to the work of education began to change. He got to know the teachers better and to see them more deeply and clearly. This surprised him, as he initially believed he was an outside influence and that his life would go on much as it had previously as priest and canon. But as his relationship to the teachers grew, he found himself getting more personally committed to them and more deeply involved in their lives and their work.

As one might imagine, this began to create a sense of disequilibrium in De La Salle's emotional life. This deepening relationship was unexpected. What did it mean? What was happening? What was he supposed to do? His focus was shifting from who he thought he was to something that was totally uncertain. And so he sought advice and wisdom from people he trusted. De La Salle never believed he was walking a path alone. He always sought the counsel of others. However, he was not always relieved by the advice he got. In this case, he might even have been shocked at what his spiritual director suggested: that De La Salle move the teachers into his home and live with them. It would be the most effective way to give them what they sorely lacked. When De La Salle accepted this wisdom, it marked the beginning of something totally new in the world—a teaching community.

The Catalyst Way

The formation of teachers continues to be a priority at Catalyst Schools. Teachers come to the school as trained and certified professionals. And of course, like any school, Catalyst offers regular professional development opportunities on a weekly basis. However, in addition to the kinds of advanced academic training that are provided in those sessions, additional time is devoted to a deeper understanding of mission and the philosophy and spirit that are the foundation stones of the school's educational work. Teachers and staff explore the *Twelve Virtues of a Good Teacher,* and engage in conversation about what it means to be Ambassadors, Guardian Angels, and Good Shepherds for their students. Teachers are often asked to witness, in formation sessions, to the way they understand and live mission. The founding story of De La Salle and the first teachers is told and retold. The success of the school depends on the culture that is established, first among the teaching community and then, through them, in the schoolwide community. Every effort is made to hire people who innately understand mission and their life as vocation, and then every effort is made to make sure they are supported and able to live it.

Community for the Sake of Mission

The core of the community that was taking shape around De La Salle was a common sense of mission and a common vision rooted in faith and Gospel values. This band of teachers were all about proclaiming the Gospel of Jesus by instilling in their students an awareness of their human dignity, the benefit of living a life guided by the Golden Rule, the good of investing back into the community from which they came, and the desire to live a full, just, and moral life. The teachers conveyed this not only through their instruction but also through personal example and selfless giving for the sake of the mission. It was for this they had joined together, and it was this De La Salle brought to their attention with such conviction that they too were persuaded that belonging to a community in educational service to youth was worth the investment of their lives. The mission, they believed, had the capacity to change not only these poor children but also the social construction of seventeenth-century French society.

These educators took their cues about community from the Gospel itself. Hold all things in common. Be fully committed. Love one another. Live simply so that others might simply live. Some committed themselves to the pursuit and implementation of the mission even if it meant they might have to live on bread alone. They claimed obedience not in a subservient way but to the mission, and all of their energy was directed to the salvation of youth through the education they provided. They thought of themselves as a social unit, a society, and they professed obedience to the needs of the group. They truly believed then, as Lasallian educators believe today, that education is the most transforming experience young people can have. This gift was worth the hardships any teacher encounters. The feeling of being tired, of not always having sufficient time, of frustration with a child who hasn't yet been reached, of not knowing how to structure an important lesson, of worrying and losing sleep over a child—every teacher feels these things. Members of this early community offered their service gratuitously and without pay. They depended on the kindness of others to a large extent, though De La Salle also found funds that helped support the enterprise. Their entire focus was the exaltation of children—raising them up and promoting their growth in goodness and practical skills. Everything was placed in service to this mission.

This fledgling society or community of teachers grew in competence and their value was seen as one town after another requested their presence in their schools. These first Lasallians opened many schools throughout France and eventually in more than eighty countries around the globe. They lived a common life for one reason—the mission. It was an intensely focused vocation. And it was viewed not as a job but as a calling. It was about an identity, not simply a set of activities. They came to be known as brothers because that was who they were to one another and to their students. De La Salle did not allow the group to grow in wealth and did not allow any of its members to join the ranks of the clergy. Wealth and clerical prestige would distract from their primary purpose. Their identity was purely and simply—teacher.

Today life is different. Societies have changed significantly and will continue to change at a rapid pace. So how important is the sense of community in the schools today?

Need for Community—Shared Mission

The sense of community the early brothers shared is crucial in today's climate and critical in educational reform. More important than any development in curriculum, any new set of standards, any code of discipline, is the person of the teacher. A teacher can have greater impact in a child's life, for good or ill, than anyone but a parent—and sometimes even more than the parent. The power of a teacher is significant.

Because the individual teacher has such personal power in a classroom, it is important that the teaching community calls each of its participants to remember that that power is to be used in service to children. Teaching is always about children. Raising children is much too significant a work to be done in isolation. It requires the adults in the system to stand together and in association with one another. It demands that there be a common vision and sense of purpose. The school is one and not divided. The educators, to be most effective, should be of one mind and heart and committed together to the mission of the school. The teachers become a united force that supports, nurtures, and challenges each member. Members of a teaching community need one another because it is in rubbing shoulders, in observing one another, in dialogue, in collaborative decision making, in mutual responsibility for all that happens, that each individual and the entire group grow and become better. We don't grow alone. We never have and we never will. Growth happens in community. Humans are social beings and we progress or fall together. It's in the DNA to desire union. While it is not always easy, it is natural and essential if we aren't to become total neurotics. Individuals achieve a sense of balance because others call them back when they are leaning too far over the edge. When one is in trouble, trusted others can offer support and help think through the presenting difficulty. Together the community faces its biggest obstacles and celebrates its success.

Joining together in this kind of association is a graphic model for children that life is a grand unity and not divided. The empathy, compassion, and love shared among the adults speaks loudly that life does not have to be as it is on the street. When the school is a functional community in this sense, it is transformative. In this sense the community of educators stands as a sacramental reality. It is a symbol of human unity and love and it is a real manifestation in the lives of students of what it symbolizes.

The leadership of the De La Salle Christian Brothers drafted a document in 1997 called *The Lasallian Mission of Human and Christian Education: A Shared Mission*. The document is a statement of recognition that the vocation of teacher is open to all who wholeheartedly embrace this common sense of mission and purpose. In speaking about the nature of the school, the authors say:

> Everything which engenders a school climate of warm relationships is an important step in achieving the school's mission. These relationships include those of the students with one another, as well as those of students with all adults and the relationships of the adults among themselves: all of this is to be marked by respect for the uniqueness of each person. (*The Lasallian Mission of Human and Christian Education: A Shared Mission*, 52, 2.12)

In a document from 1967, *A Declaration on the Brother of the Christian Schools in the World Today*, the Lasallian community stated that:

> Thus the school will be a living community where young people, coming from different social and family backgrounds, educate one another by mutual understanding and respect, openness of mind in dialogue, acceptance of the uniqueness and limitations of each, growth in the spirit of service, and the practice of justice and fraternal charity. (*A Declaration*, 46.2)

The Lasallian school, as it was intended by De La Salle, was not to be a simple source of intellectual challenge and the passing on of information but rather a school for life. The school must demonstrate that we are truly connected to one another and that each one of us has great effect on the rest. The life lived in the school speaks to how life can be lived beyond the institutional walls.

The Lasallian Mission of Human and Christian Education: A Shared Mission goes on to say:

> Values, the wise old maxim asserts, are caught rather than taught. But, to the extent that this maxim is true, it needs to be refined by suggesting that values can also be caught precisely because they are taught. That is to say, they can be acquired precisely because students see these values embodied in the attitudes and actions of their own teachers, in

the climate of the school community, and in the importance given to values in the curriculum. (64, 2.36)

Community then is not just for the sake of being friends or having a good place to come to each day. It is an intentionally created reality that serves children and asks them to embrace their best selves.

Pope Paul VI wrote, and it is important to take this to heart: "Today people listen more willingly to witnesses than to teachers, and if they listen to teachers, it is because they are witnesses."[25]

Teachers are witnesses to the way life can be. They inspire hope because they are believable not just in what they say but in who they are.

The Person of the Teacher

In many of his writings, Saint John Baptist de La Salle used deeply religious imagery to speak about the kind of relationship this community would evoke between a teacher and a student. He calls teachers Good Shepherds who know each child individually and personally and who would go to the ends of the earth to reach a troubled child. He refers to teachers as Guardian Angels who watch over their children's welfare with unrelenting diligence. He speaks about teachers as Ambassadors of Jesus Christ who announce good news. He says that teachers are like the Apostles, working tirelessly for the salvation of the young. The images he uses are personal and express an intimacy that should exist in the school between a teacher and his or her students. Before they are scholars, students are first of all children. The relationship De La Salle proposes we have with our children is profound, always for the good of the child and not our own; highly appropriate, but always personal.

There is no community without knowledge of one another. There is no community without mutual understanding. There is no community without trust and mutual respect. One might say there is no education unless we know our students, have mutual understanding, and exercise trust and respect. That's what the Lasallian community models and what we become as we find ways to build the relationships that make it possible.

We educate children together and by association—in community. Yet we never forget that every child and every teacher is unique. Community is built upon mutual respect among unique individuals who choose to hold hands for a common vision.

---

25. Pope Paul VI, *Evangelization in the Modern World,* Dec. 8, 1975, no. 41, http://w2.vatican.va/content/paul-vi/en/apost_exhortations/documents/hf_p-vi_exh_19751208_evangelii-nuntiandi.html.

Mutual Respect

De La Salle was fully conscious of the importance of treating each person with respect and of knowing individual needs. He knew that we receive from the children the permission to be their teacher because they come to believe we care about them and know them. In speaking about the essential qualities of the Good Shepherd, he says:

> One quality he must possess, according to our Savior, is to know each one of them individually. This ought also to be one of the main concerns of those who instruct others: to be able to understand their students and to discern the right way to guide them.
>
> They must show more mildness toward some, more firmness toward others. There are those who call for much patience, those who need to be stimulated and spurred on, some who need to be reproved and punished to correct them of their faults, others who must constantly be watched over to prevent them from being lost or going astray.[26]

Communities are not made up of nameless faces all marching in lockstep to the command of an autocrat. They are made of real flesh-and-blood persons each of whom deserves to be known and to whom respect is due.

In a Lasallian school this is the first and most important building block of community. Each of us is born with inherent dignity no matter our intellectual capacity, emotional development, or any gift or disability that might be part of our reality. Each of us is a person and each person is welcome and belongs. When we get beyond the superficial elements that we typically notice first, we recognize in one another that we are all fundamentally the same. Everyone has passion, desire, hope, fear, need. The ability to see beyond appearances is both critical and our calling. If education is to be effective it must be personal. If it is personal it has to be built on more than the superficial elements that govern so much of our social interactions.

Respect implies that each person is an end in and of himself or herself and not a tool to be used for some other purpose or the accomplishment of another person's goals. Each of us has inherent value that needs to be seen and upheld, nurtured and celebrated. Moreover, respect implies an understanding that people must be treated equitably, ensuring the human rights

---

26. John Baptist de La Salle, "Meditations for Sundays of the Year, 33.1," *Meditations by John Baptist de La Salle,* trans. Richard Arnandez, FSC, and Augustine Loes, FSC, vol. 4 of *Lasallian Sources: The Complete Works of Saint John Baptist de La Salle* (Lasallian Publications, 1994, reprinted 2007).

that are part and parcel of simply being human. When we build a culture of respect, each of us looks upon the other as another self and not as an object.

De La Salle possessed a heightened sense of the dignity that each child possesses and it is why he insisted that each one be known and treated as an individual, not as a member of a particular caste or as simply one among the many.

Community built upon respect for one another calls us to a deeper level of inclusivity, communication, and collaboration. Respect breeds trust. Has there ever been a true sense of community without those elements?

Of course, we know community can't be formed where trust is missing. When children don't trust teachers they become rebellious and don't enter into the appropriate learning dynamics of the class. When the teachers don't trust their administrators they function on the margins and the school suffers from a lack of cohesion around vision and mission and the strategic efforts to implement them.

Twelve Virtues of a Good Teacher: A Blueprint	
Gravity:	modest, polite; establish good order and classroom management
Silence:	speak when necessary; know what is important and what is not
Prudence:	choose appropriate means to achieve a worthy goal
Humility:	realize we have nothing that has not been given to us and we are called to share for the sake of others
Wisdom:	a deep understanding of what is worthy of our effort
Patience:	peaceful possession of our very self (self-control); right perspective
Reserve:	think, speak, and act with moderation, discretion, and modesty
Gentleness:	goodness, tenderness, sensitivity—right relationship (Note that this is the longest section in De La Salle's discussion of virtues.)
Zeal:	go the extra mile; do what is needed for the child's success
Vigilance:	diligence in all of our duties, especially watching over the well-being of children; being accountable for the stewardship entrusted to us
Reverence:	examine and be comfortable with the deepest parts of our very self and our relationship with the rest of creation and our understanding of life itself (for De La Salle this was obviously about how we manifest our commitment to faith and the Gospel)
Generosity:	sacrifice our personal interests to those of our neighbor and those in need (generosity comes from awareness that we are not the center of the universe but rather a unity in the symphony of the universe—one partner in the cosmic dance)

The Catalyst Way

At Catalyst *The Twelve Virtues of a Good Teacher* has been broken down into two- and three-page selections, interpreted for public schools, followed by questions for reflection and discussion. The Twelve Virtues are often used as a tool for mission formation during professional development when mission is the focus. Each virtue is the focus of a cluster of teachers who engage the content and articulate ways we currently live the virtue and additional ways we might live it. In these sessions participants frequently cite examples of how they see their colleagues living one or more of the virtues. Conversation need not be limited to a single formation session. One suggestion that would continue ongoing implementation in a practical way was to divide the teachers into groups that were named by the virtues. Each group would represent one of the virtues in the life of the school. That group would become responsible for calling the entire community to a deeper integration through reminders, rituals, and teaching about the specific virtue. The postscript in the document outlines the conditions for discipline to be appropriate and the code of discipline takes these conditions into account and addresses both teachers and their students. In some ways, the document can be viewed as a blueprint for relationship building in the school.

De La Salle identified the qualities and behaviors in adults that are conducive to building trust with the children entrusted to their care. Those same qualities could also help those adults build the kind of trust among themselves that promotes true community.[27]

Very briefly, this is the list of the virtues the early teaching community identified as best practice for teachers to adopt. They helped a teacher engage children appropriately, and when the teacher displayed these virtues (virtue is a habit), children more quickly became vested in their education and contributing to a healthy classroom culture.

Teachers from Chicago's west- and south-side neighborhoods gather for a teacher institute, a beginning-of-the-year in-service and mission formation.

---

27. De La Salle's understanding of these teacher qualities was codified in 1785 in a document called *The Twelve Virtues of a Good Teacher*. The full document can be found at Christian Brothers Conference Store, http://lasallianstore.com/order/lasallian-books/.

When you examine and reflect upon these qualities, it is not difficult to see how they promote healthy relationships. When we integrate them and they become part and parcel of our own behavior we are able to clearly demonstrate our respect for one another and our children and be perceived as a constructive and productive member of a team in which all the participants demonstrate this kind of concern, respect, and self-awareness.

Core Value: Concern for the Poor and Social Justice

De La Salle was a priest with a lucrative position at the Cathedral. His family had money. He initially had no inclination to involve himself in what turned into his life work. How did it happen? As he said, it was "one step at a time, imperceptibly."

In some ways De La Salle was seduced by the poor in his city and by the teachers he helped organize. His conversion came as he grew closer to the needs of the poor and his recognition of their dignity as children of God. It was the teachers and the poor who taught De La Salle abandonment to the providence of God. They boldly demanded that he walk his own talk or quit preaching trust in God to them. They knew all too well that he had personal and family wealth while they had nothing. If abandonment to God's goodness was good for them, why not for him?

Their intervention caught him by surprise and gave him pause. As a result, he decided to distribute his personal wealth to the poor and hungry during a terrible famine. In this way he became like his brothers and was no longer distinct because of his economic situation. Now he, like them, would be destitute if the mission failed. He saw the inequities in life and knew the suffering poor were not inhuman because of their poverty. He could see the systemic injustice of a society built upon the Estates, which was just a nice way to talk about a caste system. He chose to respond with education as a way to change the socially constructed inequities of his day. Relationships brought him to this point, and what De La Salle saw as the hand of God writing deeply in his heart. The school not only educated children, it was a tool for the restructuring of those systemic elements that institutionalized poverty and kept opportunity beyond the reach of so many. How? By providing the chance for a fulfilling, productive life and knowing the love of God. Lasallian schools were begun as, and continue to be, works of justice that have special preference for the economically poor.

The LaSallian Way

Lasallian schools educate more children than any other private network in the world.

Students include Christians of all denominations, as well as Jews, Muslims, Buddhists, Hindus, secularists, atheists, and agnostics. "Almost half of all students [in the United States] (19,321 students or 49 percent) requested [some] form of needs-based tuition assistance."[28]

Lasallian Network schools gave more than $80 million in need-based grants (including work study) over the 2014–2015 school year. In total, schools in the Lasallian Network gave more than $96 million in total financial aid in the 2014–2015 school year.[29]

The Catalyst Schools are a presence in communities plagued by the effects of racial discrimination, both systemic and economic. These communities are victimized by the drug trade, guns, and violence. Families struggle to lift up their children and to give them opportunity. Catalyst Schools clearly serve the economically poor—between 95 to 99 percent of the students are eligible for free or reduced lunch, an indicator of the level of poverty in the community. Because Catalyst is a public school and not part of the private Lasallian Network, their statistics are not included in the cited study.

28. Jonathon L. Wiggins, Thomas P. Gaunt, SJ, and Jonathon Holland, "Schools, Educational Centers, Youth and Family Services, and Support Ministries: *A Report for the Brothers of the Christian Schools Lasallian Region of North America (RELAN)* 2014–2015 Statistical Report," Center for Applied Research in the Apostolate, Georgetown University, Washington, DC, 31, http://www.lasallian.info/wp-content/uploads/2015/02/RELAN_2014_2015_Statistical_Report-26Feb2015.pdf.

29. Ibid., 40.

The Lasallian Story in Education

In Daniel Quinn's novel, Ishmael, one of the main characters says,

> . . . These are words that will have special meaning in our discourse here. First definition: *story.* A story is a scenario relating man, the world, and the gods. . . .
>
> Second definition: *to enact.* To enact a story is to live so as to make the story a reality. In other words, to enact a story is to strive to make it come true. . . .
>
> Third definition: *culture.* A culture is a people enacting a story.[30]

What is the story we want to enact? This seems to be the national discussion at the moment, though it's not an honest discussion. We fight over all kinds of things such as what can be taught in schools, gay marriage, immigration, America's role in world security, health care—the list goes on. We've reduced ourselves to near ideological idiocy because we won't engage honest, compassionate dialogue. There is no Socratic methodology in our relationship, so there is no legitimate truth seeking. No one intends to be changed or to learn something that might shift perspective. At the heart of this conflict is a deep disagreement about the story we want to enact. We no longer have a single story upon which to base our identity.

So what has this to do with the Lasallian school?

There are many ways to talk about justice. In its most fundamental conceptualization, social justice has everything to do with the Lasallian Story because as Lasallians, we are dedicated to developing human potential. Social justice isn't simply a disinterested and altruistic notion. When human potential is developed the talent and skill that lie within each person is made available to the rest of society. Organizing society based on the principles of social justice creates a sense of unity that reflects the unity of creation.

One way to look at justice, according to Diarmuid O'Murchu, is to view it as "radical inclusion."[31] Justice is about mutuality and inclusion. The school that thinks of itself as a work of justice is motivated to bring about the salvation of the young—offering the skill-building opportunities and the training in higher-level critical thinking, analysis, and synthesis that make mutuality possible and counter the exclusions that result from racial, economic, gender,

---

30. Daniel Quinn, *Ishmael: An Adventure of the Mind and Spirit* (New York: Bantam Turner Book, 1992), 41.

31. Diarmuid O'Murchu, *Poverty, Celibacy, and Obedience: A Radical Option for Life* (New York: Crossroad Publishing, 1999), 76.

sexual identity or any other kind of discrimination. Mutuality and inclusion are stances against violence, whether psychological, emotional, or physical. When the school is a work of justice, it is building an empathetic and inclusive community and a network of mutual support.

At a faith-based private school, or at a faith-inspired public school, the cues for establishing a just society are taken from faith. The concepts involved in understanding social justice are deeply rooted not only in politics but most especially in the faiths of the world. Search Judaism, Christianity, Hinduism, or Islam for the most significant ideas that have given rise to the modern understanding of what social justice is all about.

In both the Jewish and Christian sacred writings, as well as in the Islamic faith, who is it that always has the warm embrace of God securely wrapped around them? It is the alien, the marginalized, the poor, the downtrodden, the outcast, the leper, the prostitute, the tax collector, the lame, the despised, the elderly. It is to these that we are called to extend warmth and hospitality and charity. Religious texts establish the foundational call to charity, to care for the least among us. They also reveal that we are to challenge the systems that are unjust and that institutionalize injustice.

Insights gained from centuries of reflection on these sacred texts, combined with observation of and participation in social structures that have evolved over millennia, yield some principles of social justice that might inform administrators and educators in a Lasallian school. Seven fundamental themes that rise from such a context of faith also can serve us well in a public school.[32]

Seven Themes

Life and Dignity of the Human Person
Human life is sacred and the dignity of the human person is the foundation of a moral vision for society. . . . In our society, human life is under [constant threat and] the value of human life is [threatened in a variety of ways.] . . . Every person is precious, people are more important than things, and the measure of every institution is whether it threatens or enhances the life and dignity of the human person.[33]

---

32. The themes in italics on the pages that follow are quoted and paraphrased from "Seven Themes of Catholic Social Teaching," United States Catholic Bishops' Conference, http://www.usccb.org/beliefs-and-teachings/what-we-believe/catholic-social-teaching/seven-themes-of-catholic-social-teaching.cfm.

33. "Seven Themes of Catholic Social Teaching," United States Catholic Bishops' Conference, http://www.usccb.org/beliefs-and-teachings/what-we-believe/catholic-social-teaching/seven-themes-of-catholic-social-teaching.cfm.

How do we treat the least among us? De La Salle asked for special attention to be given to those most in need. The least among us is given preference. The pupil who can't seem to "get it," the one who has behavioral or emotional issues that frustrate us, the child who comes to school dirty—it is of these very ones that De La Salle advises us to look beyond the rags to the Christ Child within. At Catalyst this is why students with special needs always receive the attention they deserve. It is why the child of the addicted mother got a personal knock on the door by an assistant principal so he could wake up in time for school. It is why staff cleaned the uniform of a young boy who had no way to clean his own clothes. It is why there are afterschool services with programs appealing to varied student interests. It is why there are peace circles that help students in conflict see each other as real human persons. Such acts and programs demonstrate the respect, compassion, inclusion, and love that define Catalyst Schools.

Ms. Morgan, community outreach director at Catalyst Circle Rock, in the Austin neighborhood, reminds us that we make no distinction among our children. "Here everyone can come. There are no exclusions. All are welcome. We don't put anyone out. We walk the extra mile for every one of our children."

Mr. Moore, Catalyst Schools dean at Catalyst Maria in Chicago Lawn, amplifies these sentiments. "Concern for the poor ties into a quality education," he says. "Even the poorest among us deserve the very things we want for our own children."

At Catalyst, one set of behavior policies apply to all. The school uniform not only builds a sense of common and communal identity, it also eliminates dress and style as a way to separate the poor from those with more money. De La Salle made sure everyone was fed and that poverty did not impede education. Hunger is a consideration at Catalyst and everyone shares a common meal each day. These practices are not unique to Catalyst. However, they began with De La Salle's insistence that everyone be treated equally, that there be no distinction between rich and poor, that everyone receive food daily, and that the code of conduct apply to all, including those provisions governing the adult administering correction. These practices are embraced not only in the schools he founded, but also today by a wide range of schools, public and private. They are part of the tradition claimed by Catalyst.

Call to Family, Community, and Participation

The person is not only sacred but also social. How we organize our society—in economics and politics, in law and policy—directly affects human dignity and the capacity of individuals to grow in community. Marriage and the family are the central social institutions that must be supported and strengthened, not undermined. We believe people have a right and

The Catalyst Way

The very first thing that happens with a child newly enrolling at a Catalyst school is a meeting with his or her family. It is the first step in getting to know the person who will be sitting with us each day. None of us exists outside of a social setting and the child's family is the first context in which the personality, perspective on life, and world-view of the child begins to take shape. If we want to know the person within the "rags" we begin by developing a better understanding of his or her context. Each child, along with the parent or guardian, is asked about his or her goals. Diagnostic testing is used to determine the starting point for the child's academic growth. Differentiating content requires that we know the student first. Once school is underway, the symbolic ritual of the morning greeting of each student by the adults in the community indicates the desire to be in a relationship that is inclusive, mutual, and welcoming. If the teacher does not know a child, information can be passed on but real education will not occur. Education only takes place in a relationship that is supportive, and in which the child develops a respect and love for the teacher.

© John Lee, John Lee Pictures ht.

At Catalyst Schools Circle Rock Campus, as at other Catalyst Schools, uniforms are standard, building a sense of communal identity among the children.

a duty to participate in society, seeking together the common good and well-being of all, especially the poor and vulnerable. [34]

In the school inspired by the Lasallian vision, everyone belongs, community is central, and strategies that fit the circumstances and situation of the particular school are devised and implemented in order to create and demonstrate the importance of such values. High school homerooms in part shape their identity by naming themselves after outstanding universities like Harvard, Howard, or Notre Dame. At the elementary level, students are with each other seven hours every day. Elementary students have many opportunities to build a sense of community. They read together, play together, eat together, and the teachers design activities that encourage collaboration and team effort.

Rights and Responsibilities
Human dignity can be protected and a healthy community can be achieved only if human rights are protected and responsibilities are met. Therefore, every person has a fundamental right to life and a right to those things required for human decency. Corresponding to these rights are duties and responsibilities—to one another, to our families, and to the larger society. [35]

The Lasallian school is never a one-way street, with some people doing all the giving and others all the receiving. It is a place where mutual commitments are made explicit and the norm. Teachers and administrators are competent, prepared, and skilled, and students give their all through hard work and genuine concern not only for their personal success, but also the success of their classmates. The school is a training ground for life beyond graduation.

Option for the Poor and Vulnerable
A basic moral test is how our most vulnerable members are faring. In a society marred by deepening divisions between rich and poor, our tradition recalls the story of the Last Judgment (Mt 25:31–46) and instructs us to put the needs of the poor and vulnerable first. [36]

This is why De La Salle became so deeply involved in the movement he founded. He was well aware of the failure of his own social structures to uphold the dignity of the most vulnerable. The class and economic structures

---

34. Ibid.

35. Ibid.

36. Ibid.

The Catalyst Way

Community does not only happen in the classroom. Extra-curricular activities are purposefully designed to advance community. Catalyst's approach to the young women in the school provides one example of this community building. Groups are formed in which a trusted adult works with girls regarding self-image, relationships with boys, and the cultural images of women (positive and negative) that they are trying to live into. Overnight retreat experiences provide opportunities for girls to bond and actively participate. Athletics are not the only kinds of teams at Catalyst. While sports are important, so are the arts. This is why ninety students have joined the Ravinia Circle Rockets orchestra. It is why students are invited to participate in writing and reciting poetry. It is why student art decorates the halls near the art room. Faculty and staff engage students according to their natural talents and interests and actively nurture their growth.

were destructive of family life and the children were the most vulnerable. This reality is repeated in our own time. People need to work from morning to night with little energy left for what many would say are some of the most important things in life, such as significant relationships and activities that help develop our human potential. Many work hard and long hours at minimum wage jobs without benefits. They are trapped in the cycle of poverty and have no apparent way out. And it is children who continue to suffer as a result. When the choice in the winter, for the working poor, is between food and heat there is something wrong with how we are caring for the least among us. Education in this context is definitely a work of justice. It is, for educators, a way to carve a path out of poverty and to create right relationship in our society.

The Dignity of Work and the Rights of Workers

The economy must serve people, not the other way around. Work is more than a way to make a living; it is a form of continuing participation in God's creation. If the dignity of work is to be protected, then the basic rights of workers must be respected—the right to productive work, to decent and fair wages, to the organization and joining of unions, to private property, and to economic initiative.[37]

In Lasallian schools the work force is respected. Teaching is a difficult challenge under the best of circumstances and educators are on the go from early morning till late in the evening. Teachers must balance a multitude of relationships and responsibilities. Work-life balance is always a tension, especially for those who have primary relationships beyond the school—partners, families, good friends—all of whom need and deserve the educator's presence in their lives. Unnecessary burdens are not laid upon the shoulders of those who are the frontline mission bearers, those most directly in relationship with children. Administrators regularly recognize and demonstrate appreciation for teachers and other staff.

Catalyst Schools strive to provide the benefits and safety nets that support the entire team. Often, the notion of a union frightens administrators yet educators have every right to associate and to establish a common voice for their legitimate concerns. However, if the school is a real community, if everyone's voice is given real hearing, if leadership is shared, if legitimate authority is participative, if there is a common sense of mission and vision, if the dignity and rights of each person are respected, the union is of mind and heart because legitimate concerns are always heard and addressed. The school is a workplace that must serve people, which includes the educational team and never the other way around. Everyone is there for the same reason—the flourishing and salvation of the young.

There need be no unresolvable conflict over rights and responsibilities when mission is always the primary focus and systems are put in place to make sure communication is open and invited, and respect is mutually given and received.

Solidarity

We are one human family whatever our national, racial, ethnic, economic, and ideological differences. We are our brothers and sisters keepers, wherever they may be. Loving our neighbor has global dimensions in a shrinking world. At the core of the virtue of solidarity is the pursuit of justice and peace. Pope Paul VI taught that if you want peace, work for

---

37. Ibid.

justice. The Gospel calls us to be peacemakers. Our love for all our sisters and brothers demands that we promote peace in a world surrounded by violence and conflict.[38]

De La Salle was challenged by his teachers, his brothers, to walk his talk. Basically this meant demonstrating a deep sense of solidarity with the poor. De La Salle taught his teachers to trust in the Providence of God. He spoke about the birds of the air and the flowers in the field and how God takes care of these—so they should not worry about their physical welfare. The teachers were well aware of De La Salle's financial security. They rightly pointed out that these things were easy for him to say but that they were the one's living what he taught, and it seemed to them that he was not. He had a significant cushion that would catch him should the enterprise fail.

De La Salle knew in his heart that the sense of solidarity they were challenging him to embrace was necessary. So he distributed his wealth to the poor during a famine and retained only enough so that he would not be a burden upon the fledgling community. He joined the ranks of those who depended upon Providence and left the ranks of those who only preach about it. In our schools, we might also ask ourselves what we know about those we serve. An awareness of their life challenges and the consequences of disenfranchisement and poverty imposed upon them gives us great insight into the nature of the children entrusted to our care. Such knowledge teaches the teacher how to better reach her or his students. It also calls us to align ourselves with those who work tirelessly to change the very structures that have institutionalized the poverty we witness each day in our children. Standing in solidarity with the poor means we understand the communities in which we serve. It is incredibly difficult to be one with people we do not know and when we allow a great distance to exist between us.

Care for Creation
We show respect by our stewardship of creation. Care for the earth is not just an Earth Day slogan, it is a requirement of our faith. We are called to protect people and the planet, living our faith in relationship with all of God's creation. This environmental challenge has fundamental moral and ethical dimensions that cannot be ignored.[39]

---

38. Ibid. The teaching by Pope Paul VI is from *Message for the Celebration of the Day of Peace, 1 January 1972*, http://w2.vatican.va/content/paul-vi/en/messages/peace/documents/hf_p-vi_mes_19711208_v-world-day-for-peace.html.

39. Ibid.

If life is indeed a grand unity, then it makes sense to take seriously our responsibility for all of life. Science demonstrates that the stuff of the stars is the very stuff of which we are made. Life is an organic whole and humanity is not separate from the rest of the universe. We are part of it, moving through space on one small globe just like the other planets and stars. Caring for all of creation is caring for our very selves. When we abuse our resources, we set ourselves up for disaster. Human consciousness gives us the opportunity to reflect on what we see and experience. That pondering, wondering, the search for meaning, leads us to the awe, gratitude, and trust that are the foundation stones of faith and the basics of life's very mystery that lies at the heart of who we are.

Organizing our corporate life around these principles and teaching them offers students a preparation for moral life in the world. These seven principles can become an axis around how graduates generate their life's work, organize their businesses, interact with those still living in poverty, establish government policy, or manage and supervise others. They should also learn their rights and be convinced of their own dignity and worth. We offer them a coherent way of understanding themselves and their relationship to the rest of life through our teaching and our example.

Civil Rights

The explosive and dynamic civil rights movement of the 1960s grew from the ground up. David Halberstam, in his book *The Children*, demonstrates the power of education as he recounts the story of the march for civil rights. The very cover of his book says:

> On the first day of the sit-ins, in Nashville, Tennessee, eight young black college students found themselves propelled into the leadership of the civil rights movement, as the movement—and America—entered a period of dramatic change. The courage and vision of these young people changed history.[40]

Young college students ultimately led the civil rights movement. Teachers like Jim Lawson and Kelly Miller Smith, and others, activated the imaginations and the dreams of a better society in these students.

Education was the cornerstone of the movement that gave rise to Martin Luther King, Jr., Ralph Abernathy, John Lewis, and the other prominent

---

40. David Halberstam, *The Children* (New York and Toronto: A Fawcett Book, Random House Publishing Group, 1998).

leaders who rallied the nation in support of civil rights. The faith-based non-violence they advocated in the face of horrible abuse won the hearts of a nation. It was education and faith that brought the savagery of abuse rampant in the lives of African American citizens to light and created the path to a more just society.

The fact is, however, racism still exists, as do the unjust systems that have, in many ways, institutionalized it. People of color still live as second-class citizens, as do other minority groups. We talk constantly about the achievement gap in education, the lack of employment opportunities in minority communities in general, the social and business ceilings that cannot yet be broken. Maybe discrimination is more subtle, since today anyone can sit at a lunch counter. But the mostly white, straight, male majority still controls all the institutional structures that provide the benefits they themselves so richly enjoy while shortchanging so many others.

Education Is a Way Out

The first line of defense might be drawn anywhere—more cohesive, value-based families, regulation of business, affirmative action, laws against redlining—but education must be considered one of the core elements required for social justice, social change, and civil rights to continue moving forward, as well as for the advancement of the entire society.

Education is the first step out of poverty. Getting children through elementary and secondary education and into university provides a wealth of opportunity that those without that education will never enjoy. That's why the Lasallian school takes the long view. The goal is not a particular test score. The goal is a productive, moral life. When do we claim success? We claim success when we can say our graduates are making a contribution to the communities in which they live and work. We claim success when we can say our graduates are enhancing the lives of others. We claim success when our graduates assume adult responsibility, exercise a mature conscience, and have the demonstrated capacity to care for themselves.

the Catalyst Way

*C*atalyst is only nine years old. According to the school's website, 97 percent of high school-age graduates from Catalyst Circle Rock and Catalyst Howland "are currently enrolled and on-track to graduate from high school within four years." Catalyst Maria, on Chicago's south side and educating students from Chicago Lawn and Englewood, has placed 100 percent of its graduates in either junior or four-year colleges. (Check the website for additional information, http://catalystschools.org/.) While they have not advanced to the level of assuming adult responsibility yet, ongoing relationships and follow-up communication with these young men and women will reveal the level of the school's success over time, as it is discovered how they have advanced in their education, their careers, and the degree to which they have become contributing members of their communities.

© Miike Fehrenbach, FSC

Eighth-grade graduates from Catalyst Circle Rock Charter School proudly point to their diplomas. Ninety-seven percent of Catalyst Circle Rock and Catalyst Howland charter schools graduates are on track to graduate from high school within four years.

Even at the most basic level—income disparity—we know:

> There is a clear correlation between a person's educational attainment and his or her earning power. And that link is growing stronger by the year, as shown by a series of U.S. Census Bureau reports since 1975:
> Adults with bachelor's degrees in the late 1970s earned 55 percent more than adults who had not advanced beyond high school. That gap grew to 75 percent by 1990—and is now at 85 percent.[41]

When we can raise a family's earning power through better education and teaching how to take advantage of life opportunities, the entire social system is better, with one caveat: that we also help develop a sense of social responsibility, a moral compass, and a mature sense of conscience that guides people into right relationship.

A wise man once said that as long as I resent you and put my foot on you to keep you lying in the gutter, we are both stuck and unable to advance. There is no movement. There is no profit in holding others back. There is also no profit in hanging on to anger, hate, and the desire for revenge. Both are like the sticky mousetraps that glue the rodent in misery without actually ending its life. When we recognize the humanity and dignity of every person and demonstrate respect we move forward. When we learn to let go of our hurt and to forgive we move forward. The infliction of injustice and our inability to forgive both mean a spiral into dysfunctional ways of living that greatly reduce the joy that could be at the center of life.

We could be well advised to heed the scriptural admonitions—die to self and forgive seventy times seven.

---

41. G. Scott Thomas, "Earnings Widen Between College and High School-only Grads," *The Business Journals,* Dec. 28, 2012, http://www.bizjournals.com/bizjournals/on-numbers/scott-thomas/2012/12/grads-earn-85-more-than-those-without.html?page=all. It is worth noting that despite the added earning potential over time that accompanies a college degree, a recent study suggests that minorities, even with a college degree, and notably blacks and Latinos, nonetheless suffer more than other racial and ethnic groups when economic times are rough (http://www.cssny.org/news/entry/report-barriers-remain-for-college-educated-blacks-and-latinos).

4 Core Partnerships

Volunteers install a playground at Catalyst Maria Charter School in the Chicago Lawn neighborhood.

An important concept as expressed in the work and writings of De La Salle and the original group of teachers was the significance of association and community. Their lives were organized around the idea that life in community is a most effective way to accomplish such an important social mission as the education of youth.

De La Salle and his teachers lived together. This was how they developed one mind and one heart for the mission of the schools. The sense of community was deeper than simply living together, however. It encompassed the entire enterprise they shared and was not isolated or simply internal. Life in community was not for the sake of the community itself but rather it was for the sake of mission. It included their sense of unity with the children and the great benefit education was for entire families and society.

The very words the early teachers used in expressing their commitment were "together and by association" and "for the sake of." The "for the sake of" was their mission of education as a means to save poor children. The teachers clearly recognized that we own and implement this mission together and not alone. For De La Salle and the early teaching community, their own salvation was intimately connected with the work they did for children. The sacrifices they made in the school, the hunger and cold they may have experienced, helped create strong bonds between them and with their students. Living was sacrificial in order that the mission would thrive.

For De La Salle the religious context of his life provided the metaphor for a deep understanding of what this unity should be. His notion of the vine and the branches spoke to what sustained the community in good times and in bad. Union with the source, God for De La Salle, provided the sustenance and nurture that kept the group alive when all physical evidence would indicate it should whither. When we stay connected we grow and live. When we get cut off, we die. The same is true today. When we are connected to those things that support and nurture us, that are life-sustaining, that deepen our sense of humanity, we thrive. Cut us off from those things and we suffer both physically and emotionally.

This image of vine and branches remains useful when we consider the great import of the mission we share. When we stay connected to that sense of life purpose and to one another we grow and live. When we stay connected to our purpose and one another we thrive. The passion of the community for participation in giving life and opportunity to children is contagious. It is being attached to mission and one another that sustains us.

Today the Lasallian community talks about association. This concept comes from the research, study, and dialogue among the international Lasallian network. It is about ownership of the mission and how we participate together to provide the means for saving children.

None of us, no matter how smart, no matter how skilled, no matter how talented, no matter how motivated for good can do it alone. The operation of a successful school is a group effort. But not just any group can pull it off. It must be a group that shares a commitment to the foundational vision and the mission. Association means that we work in unity, respectful of each person, considering his or her unique individuality, talents, skills, and perspectives. Ours is a group that builds trust. On the basis of that trust a deep and abiding sense of community grows. Each person brings a unique gift into our life. When we stop and really see who each person is we ready ourselves to receive that gift. Imagine a community in which each person is ready to give and each person is ready to receive. What kind of model is that group for children? What more can children learn from us beyond the academic content that in itself is a rich blessing?

One key understanding is that no one person brings what every child needs. Our own experience as students demonstrates that some are more easily attracted to and trusting of one teacher than another. Personality, life experience, and a multitude of other human factors naturally draw us to some people rather than others. It is the community that affords the student body the variety of persons that helps make the school a comfortable and safe space in which to participate for both students and teachers.

This is the first of the core partnerships that the Lasallian tradition implies. We are associated together for the sake of the mission. We come as a full human person. We are not pretending to care, to be passionate about our work, but we are really our true selves. Ours is a real world where roles are at the service of the mission and not something to be hung onto. It is a union of equals who share an understanding of what their purpose is.

The ownership for the educational process generated through this sense of unity and appreciation for one another is a gift. It is an asset that makes the school a value to the community because it elevates the community's greatest good, the children.

At the same time the school is an asset to the community because of what it does for children, it also needs to be the community's school. It is important that parents have a sense of ownership for the mission of the school and participate in it. This is a second important partnership. To foster this second core partnership, the school—administrators, teachers, and staff—welcomes the presence and involvement of parents and families and explores ways to help build the relationship between all school personnel and the families of the students.

Research indicates children learn best when parents or guardians understand the mission and goals of the school. The research further suggests children do better when there are books in a home and parents encourage good study habits, check homework, participate in school activities with their children, check progress reports or report cards, and limit television viewing and use of social media.

What keeps any of us returning to a mechanic, a department store, a grocery? Convenience alone won't do it, although that might be part of the reason. More deeply it is because of trust. The mechanic has never lied to us, never overcharged us or done an unnecessary repair. It is this trust and the effort to extend hospitality that draw us back. It is rare that we have a family doctor we do not trust, who keeps us waiting for hours, who does not take an interest in us or talk to us about our presenting problem and offer

Parents discuss their children and educational matters at the Parent University Catalyst Howland.

a treatment plan. A restaurant in which staff demonstrate they do not need our business, that rushes us through our meal, or that provides poor service does not win our favor or our return business. Why would we think a school is different?

The kind of trust we build with our students must extend to their families. If families are to develop a sense of ownership for the school, they must feel there is good communication, a deep sense of welcome and hospitality, an ear that listens to and hears their concerns. Not every parent will even begin to avail themselves of the opportunity to be in relationship with the personnel at the school, including their child's teacher. It is important to understand why that might be the case because indifference alone may not explain it. It could be work, problems with transportation, or issues totally beyond anyone's control. Once we understand more about why a particular parent or guardian is absent from their child's school life, we might find a better way to communicate. As we differentiate education with children, we might consider how to differentiate for parents. A one-size relationship does not always fit everyone. We are convinced that parents who are actively engaged in the education of their children make a difference in their children's progress. The school and the family ought to reinforce each other's values and goals for the sake of the salvation of each child.

The Catalyst Way

There are many ways to communicate with and win the participation of families. For example, teachers can make regular positive phone calls to a child's home rather than the occasional call reporting misbehavior or a problem. Regular newsletters and notes from administrators and teachers can be helpful. Use of social media such as websites and Facebook to report school activities can be an easy, regular way to communicate with parents who use a computer or mobile phone. Family math, reading, or science nights bring many families to the school. Father-son/mother-daughter nights provide unique opportunities to bring people closer together. Athletic events typically draw families to the school. Student-led conferences, in which the child leads the discussion about the successes and challenges he or she is experiencing, provide an opportunity for a student to do a public presentation and for parents to hear their child in a more professional context. Parent breakfasts or lunches, holiday parties, and other social events can bring families to the school.

Does a school ever score 100 percent for parent and family involvement? According to the Catalyst website, "90 percent is the average parent attendance at parent meetings. Parents and families are an integral part of the Catalyst Schools mission, with monthly outreach events and informational/recreational opportunities for parents to play an integral role in their scholar's education. From quarterly Progress Report check-ins to daily interactions with teachers and staff, the education of a Catalyst scholar is one that is facilitated in partnership with families at home and at school."

This entry in a recent Catalyst e-newsletter indicates nicely how the school engages parents.

the catalyst schools

What are you a catalyst for?

Catalyst Circle Rock Parent Week

© Mike Fehrenbach, FSC

A father reads with his child during Dr. Seuss Night at Catalyst Maria.

Catalyst Circle Rock had an AMAZING Parent Week this week, with events including a Breast Cancer Awareness event, "Meet and Greet" breakfasts, and sessions on working with parents about the instructional technology programs Catalyst uses daily. A HUGE shout out to Mrs. Myers and the Catalyst team for coordinating these incredible events!

Catalyst Circle Rock had an AMAZING Parent Week this week, with events including a Breast Cancer Awareness event, "Meet and Greet" breakfasts, and sessions on working with parents about the instructional technology programs Catalyst uses daily. A HUGE shout out to Mrs. Myers and the Catalyst team for coordinating these incredible events!

A passion for parents and families, a sense of hospitality and openness, and creativity are the fundamental tools needed to be engaging. It also helps to have a school staff member whose role is parental engagement to help lead the team in this effort.

A third kind of core partnership exists between the school and other agencies dedicated to the good of the community. This is why it is important to bring the community into the school, and why the educational team at the school needs to understand the community in which it is located. Children are not isolated from their families or their community. Education takes place in a context and that context can provide valuable partnerships that enhance the education of each child.

Parents and guardians provide the appropriate guidance in the home when they understand the goals of the school and buy into them. Community agencies that understand and appreciate the value of the school to the neighborhood can also bring gifts beyond what the school alone might be able to offer. If the school is dedicated to the education of the whole child, it needs help. It is a rare school that has every resource to develop all the talents and skills of each child. It is a rare school that can instill values without the collaboration of the entire community. In fact, even though it has become the object of ridicule and satire, the notion that it takes a community to raise a child is in fact true.

Understand the context in which the school exists. Know the other assets in the community. There are politicians and political groups, community arts associations, musicians and orchestras, athletic teams and organizations, banks and other financial groups, industries and manufacturers, community service agencies like legal aide, health organizations, and churches that all have resources. Such individuals and organizations are also assets in the community and want to see positive developments and growth where they live, which is alongside the school. When school and community are engaged and relationships built between them, amazing things can happen.

A fourth kind of partnership is that between Catalyst and other educational institutions such as local colleges and universities. Benefits to Catalyst staff and students include teacher training and professional development, reduced-cost degrees, consultants, dual-credit courses, camps, campus visits, and a variety of other gifts. The Lasallian school is not simply on the receiving end of this equation. The symbiotic relationship enhances the mission of all the educational institutions involved. Catalyst provides colleges a place for urban plunges, placement of interns and practice teachers, counseling practicums, marketing design and financial projects. Everyone benefits.

The Catalyst Way

At Catalyst, the Joffrey Ballet taught first graders to dance and invited eighteen of them to join their ballet school. Ravinia, one of the premier music venues in the country, has taught kindergartners and first-graders at Catalyst to sing. In partnership with Catalyst, Ravinia established the largest African American student symphony in the country at Catalyst, with ninety young musicians. The Blackstar project has brought Catalyst fathers a deeper understanding of the need for parental engagement with children. May I Have This Dance instructors have led students to repeated first-place wins in the city ballroom dance competition. Other groups such as Poetry Slam, Written Word, theater groups, chefs who teach healthy cooking and healthy eating, banks that teach financial literacy, multiple professionals participating in career days—all have brought a world of wonderful things to our children. Community partnerships like these bring something the school cannot achieve alone. A deeper sense of community beyond the walls, and a deeper sense of ownership for the goals and purpose of the school by these outside groups, help the school become a community anchor and also draw parents and families into the mix. These partnerships bind us to the community in unique ways that always benefit the children.

The Catalyst Way

*I*n our neighborhoods:

- Only 39 percent of African American boys and 57 percent of African American girls graduate from high school by age 19.

- More than half of all households with children live in poverty.

- More than 50 percent of the adult population over 25 does not have a high school diploma.

- 94 percent of Catalyst families qualify for the free/reduced meal program.

The Catalyst Schools seek to become an anchor as well as a change agent in our neighborhoods. Each school invites families to get involved through hosting programs or volunteering as tutors and mentors. We also team up with community partners through our Renaissance Enrichment Program, which offers children classes in the arts, including dance and gospel singing, etiquette, nutrition, money management, and athletics.

De La Salle was not an isolationist. He listened to his community and his community was larger than his teachers. He valued the gifts that others brought to the table. Trusted donors, friends, and spiritual guides had ongoing and lasting importance to him. De La Salle was always both teacher and learner and knew that the work could not be done except by a community that was engaging and committed—and this community was inclusive. It would be a mistake to think such an endeavor could be taken on alone.

Some of the Catalyst Schools' Neighborhood Partners

Future "Adopt-a-Class" Program — Connects business owners and other professionals who have achieved success as entrepreneurs/professionals with students and provides one-on-one interaction.

Life Skills "Luncheon Series" Prevention Force Family Center— Presents workshops about youth violence, stress management, problem solving, and self-esteem.

Lady Mentoring Program— After-school program designed by Westside Health Authority, with topics concerning conflict management, mentoring, and leadership development.

Dominican Service Learning— Students from Dominican University provide meaningful service by tutoring Catalyst students or performing other services for students at the Catalyst Schools.

A final consideration is a fifth type of partnership. A faith-inspired public school must abide by the First Amendment protection against a state-sponsored religion. Neutrality in matters of religion is the law and must be given more than lip service. It must be a fact of life. To be a public school rooted in the values of faith is still to be a public school. There is no proselytizing, no religion classes, no religious services, no subtle influence by the adults over the children in matters of faith or adherence to religious practice or doctrine.

A relationship with a faith-based institution provides an opportunity to bring services into the mix without compromising these First Amendment protections. While the school provides the experience of faith rather than the language of religious expression and teaches the value content rather than name the values as coming from a set of sacred texts, the faith-based institution can offer wraparound services that speak more explicit religious language without hesitation. These wraparound services can also provide other programming that enhances the experience the school initiates. Retreats, communal reflection in a faith context, tutoring, community building, peace circles, conflict resolution training, and additional service projects, can be freely designed and implemented at the faith-based institution without violating the separation of church and state.

Two examples might provide insight. At one of the Catalyst Schools there is a relationship with Rock of Our Salvation Free Evangelical Church and Circle Urban Ministries. The church and the ministries outreach provide after-school programs for youth. Many but not all Catalyst families choose to send their children to these wrap-around programs, which include tutoring, college readiness programs, Scripture study, Bible camps, and some recreational programs.

Another of the Catalyst Schools has a relationship with the Maria Kaupas Center. Rooted in Catholicism, the center offers opportunities for daily reflection, retreat experiences, community building, peace circles, programs for restorative justice and community service, as well as quiet spaces for study and recreational activities.

Outreach at Catalyst's faith-based partners—the Maria Kaupas Center, Rock Church, and Circle Urban Ministries—doesn't begin and end with the schools. These organizations strive to be anchors in the community at large. Circle Urban Ministries has been deeply involved in housing issues, for example, for thirty years prior to the opening of our school. These faith-based organizations with which the schools partner also share a relationship of trust with the larger community, a relationship that by extension gives the schools additional status in the community as well.

A Word of Caution

Regarding this partnership with faith-based groups, there are some critical things to keep in mind.

First, the wraparound services are provided by some other organization, not the school. The school cannot support the services either financially or with personnel. Crossing the line would be violating the First Amendment because the school would no longer be neutral in matters of religion. Public money cannot fund religious activity.

A more subtle rationale for the noninvolvement of school personnel at the wraparound program is that young children who experience their teachers both in the classroom and then as leaders of religious activities cannot distinguish between these roles.

Second, student participation in these wraparound programs is strictly voluntary. It is something that parents and children choose. There is no coercion and no expectation that anyone take advantage of these programs. The wraparound services must "sell" themselves to parents on their own merits. It is clear to everyone that the school is distinct and separate.

What happens because these services exist, however, is the deepening of a culture of community built on respect. Children have a place to give voice to things they might not say in school because the context is different. For example, one young lady, a junior in high school, spoke of the reflection that takes place in the chapel. She said the chapel is critical to her because it is like her diary. It is where she feels free to voice her joys, her fears, her grief, and to do so in a religious context that somehow gives her strength. Other young boys and girls speak about the context of the wraparound service as a safe space in which they can hang out with friends and enjoy the company of people they care about without the kind of structure they experience in school.

It is important to be as deliberate about who the school partners with for such services as it is about who is hired as a principal or what programs the school implements. After-school services should not be an afterthought but part of the planning process. It is important to choose partners well and to make sure the structured relationship is consistent with the public schools' responsibility to remain neutral in matters of religion and faith.

In the case of all external partnerships, whether with community agencies, educational institutions, or faith-based groups, building the relationship takes time and involves false starts, negotiation, and ongoing dialogue. These are important relationships and they take time and energy.

Conclusion

Children exit the Catalyst Schools Circle Rock Charter following the first day of a new school year.

The initial question was "is it possible to operate a public school that is faith inspired and that comes out of the Lasallian tradition, a tradition deeply rooted in the Christian Gospel?"

Building the school culture around **FIVE CORE VALUES** provides a clue as to how this can be done. To be faith inspired does not mean preaching, evangelizing, or proselytizing in an effort to gain adherents to particular doctrinal statements or beliefs. To be faith inspired does not mean we are bound to a particular set of acceptable words recognized by the hierarchy of a particular faith tradition.

What this extended reflection suggests is that while public schools are secular and religion/faith neutral, there are values embedded in faith traditions that can be shared even in a public school that must adhere to the First Amendment.

First, **faith** is an experience in which a person walks into the mystery that lies at the heart of life. Mystery is not simply that which cannot be explained. Rather, mystery is that which is infinitely comprehensible. The deeper we walk into it, the further we can continue to go. Creating this sense of awe is very significant in a Lasallian school. Introducing children to wonder about the meaning of their existence prepares them for their life-long journey, which for many might become a journey of faith, and for others will simply be the journey into the wonderful gift that life is—a gift that invokes gratitude for its magnanimity and our participation in it. This is also a journey built on a sense of trust that first happens, for some children, between the child and the teacher. This relationship becomes a sacrament of the reality that life is good and trustworthy and the mystery at the heart of life is good and trustworthy as well.

Second, the **values** that come to us through the **Gospel** are worth sharing. Simply because they are embedded in sacred texts does not eliminate these values from consideration and integration into our lives. These are the very values that build a solid sense of respect and unity among peoples and between humanity and the earth upon which we depend for life. Quite possibly these values are sacred because they are first so intimately human.

Third, there is no point running a school if **academic excellence** isn't the goal. But it is important to keep in mind that academic excellence means much more than course content or academic structure and discipline. It also involves the quality of relationship between teachers and students and among the adults in the educational community of the school, as well as between the school and the community in which it serves. Most important it means an excellent teacher who understands and embraces the mission in every classroom.

Fourth, **inclusive community and respect** are the primary foundation stones for the culture of the school, and out of these characteristics so many other necessary principles flow. Without respect, without collaborative work, without knowing each other as persons beyond roles, there is no possibility that community will be established. It is coming together for the sake of children that motivates the Lasallian community.

Fifth, the Lasallian school is a work of justice. **A preference for the poor,** the disenfranchised, the marginalized children of society defines who we are. The school becomes a vehicle through which we give the young and their communities a voice. Teaching those critical thinking and other higher-level skills offers an avenue to challenge those structures and systems that institutionalize injustice in the world. The school is about civil rights, human rights, and empowerment.

Finally, it is important to remember why De La Salle began the schools in the first place. He was committed to the salvation of the young. In his context, Catholic France, the schools were faith based and specifically about the saving power of Jesus and the Gospel that flowed from the experience of his Apostles and followers. Saint John Baptist de La Salle considered salvation from a dual perspective, and both parts were important. Without one, salvation was not complete. First, it was imperative that Lasallian teachers lead children to the values of the Gospel and faith. Children had to first be good people who had a moral compass that guided their behavior and relationships. Second, De La Salle's teachers had to provide children the skills needed for a satisfying and purposeful life through which they could sustain themselves and a family as well as become productive, contributing citizens.

When we walk into the world of public education with the intent to make the school Lasallian, these five principles need to be considered, evaluated, and their implementation strategically planned.